SIRHOWY VALLEY LINE

Vic Mitchell and Keith Smith
in association with **Dave Edge**

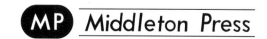

MP Middleton Press

Front cover: The end is nigh as an ex-GWR Pannier tank waits at the junction signals at Risca in about 1959. Trains for the Sirhowy Valley turned left here. (P.Chancellor coll.)

Back cover: Ex-LMS 0-8-0 no. 49064 was still fitted for winter work on 8th August 1959, as it stood near Tredegar Colliers Platform. It is coupled to no. 41204 and they were the last LMS engines to be shedded at Tredegar. (S.Rickard/J&J coll.)

Published August 2007

ISBN 978 1 906008 12 3

© Middleton Press, 2007

Design Deborah Esher
Typesetting Barbara Mitchell

Published by
       Middleton Press
       Easebourne Lane
       Midhurst
       West Sussex
       GU29 9AZ
Tel: 01730 813169
Fax: 01730 812601
Email: info@middletonpress.co.uk
www.middletonpress.co.uk

Printed & bound by Biddles Ltd, Kings Lynn

INDEX

ACKNOWLEDGEMENTS

We are very grateful for the assistance received from many of those mentioned in the credits also to W.R.Burton, A.R.Carder, D.B.Clayton, L.Crosier, G.Croughton, F.Hornby, N.Langridge, B.Lewis, Mr D. and Dr S.Salter, T.Walsh, and in particular our wives, Barbara Mitchell and Janet Smith.

I. The Sirhowy Valley line is the left one on this 1939 map. (Railway Magazine)

Reference:—
- L.M.S.R. (Sirhowy)
- Original Course of Sirhowy Tramroad
- Other L.M.S.R. Lines
- G.W.R
- Joint Lines
- Other Lines

GEOGRAPHICAL SETTING

Our route began to develop in the era of the canals in the late 18th century, when they were mainly concerned with the transport of coal and iron. Situated at the confluence of the Ebbw River and the River Usk, the docks were developed south of the wharves on the Usk and both grew greatly with the advent of the railways.

The Monmouthshire Canal ran close to the Ebbw River between Newport and Crumlin, tramroads continuing northwards in the narrowing and steepening valleys of the Ebbw Fach to Blaina, the Ebbw Fawr to Ebbw Vale and the Sirhowy to Tredegar.

The route between Newport and Risca crosses mainly sandstone, but at the latter place it entered an area of complex geology on the eastern flank of the South Wales coalfield. The line served numerous collieries.

The maps are to the scale of 25ins to 1 mile, with north at the top, unless otherwise indicated.

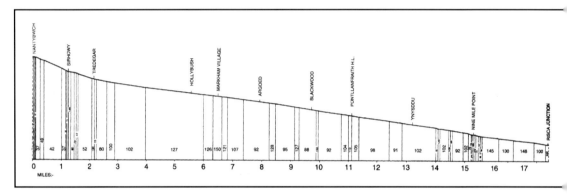

II. Gradient profile above Risca.

HISTORICAL BACKGROUND

The first "Rail Ways" in the area, more properly termed tramroads, were laid as extensions of the western arm of the Monmouthshire Canal, opened in 1796. A tramroad from the head of the canal at Crumlin to the Beaufort Iron Works at Ebbw Vale opened at about the same time. The Monmouthshire Canal Company was established by an Act of 1792, its name being changed to the Monmouthshire Railway & Canal Company in 1849. The MCC was empowered by an Act of 1802 to make further tramroads from Nine Mile Point (whence the Sirhowy Tramroad ran northwards to the ironworks of that name) to Newport, and Crumlin to Risca, to join that from Nine Mile Point. Where the line ran through Tredegar Park near Newport, it was built at the expense of the estate, which charged tolls for its use; this section was eventually purchased in 1923. The tramways ran to wharves on the banks of the River Usk, south of Newport. These lines opened around 1805 and were available for general goods traffic from 1811.

Other mineral lines in the area included Hall's Tramroad and the Aberbeeg Tramroad. The former was completed in about 1805 and ran north from Cross Keys and crossed to the Sirhowy Valley at Pentwynmawr. The latter ran through Blaina to Brynmawr, the northern part becoming known as the Llanarth Tramroad.

Newport had the benefit of broad gauge trains (7ft 0¼ins) from 18th June 1850, when the South Wales Railway opened between Chepstow and Swansea.

The MRCC relaid its line with a combination of standard gauge/tramroad track, steam and horse traction being used between about 1830 and 1849. A timetabled passenger service started on 21st December 1850 between Newport (Court-y-Bella) and Blaina. An extension to Newport Dock Street followed on 4th April 1852. The Sirhowy Tramroad construction started at its northern end in 1797. Some passengers were being conveyed by 1851.

Conversion of the tramroad was completed in 1860, but scheduled passenger service to the Sirhowy Valley did not begin until 19th June 1865. Services were extended from Sirhowy to Nantybwch on 2nd November 1868. The London & North Western Railway acquired the Sirhowy Railway under an Act dated 13th July 1876. The MRCC had two termini in Newport: Dock Street and Mill Street, and a connection between them was completed in 1855.

Brynmawr had received trains from Abergavenny from September 1862, the service being extended to Nantybwch in March 1864. The Heads of the Valleys line opened westwards in 1871-73 and the route became part of the LNWR, although joint with the Rhymney Railway in part.

The Great Western Railway and the SWR were amalgamated in 1862 and broad gauge operation in the area ceased in 1872.

The MRCC became part of the GWR in 1880 and Western Valleys services were transferred from Newport Dock Street to the main line station at High Street from 1st August of that year.

The GWR formed the Western Region of British Railways upon nationalisation in 1948. The LNWR had become a constituent of the London Midland & Scottish Railway in 1923, most of which formed the London Midland Region of BR. The Sirhowy Valley line was transferred to the WR during 1948.

Passenger service was withdrawn from the route on 13th June 1960, but Western Valleys trains served the Newport to Risca section until 30th April 1962.

Freight ceased in stages in 1960-70 and details are given in the captions.

PASSENGER SERVICES

Until about 1880, there were generally three trains between Newport and Sirhowy (two on Sundays), with four or five between Tredegar and Nantybwch (two on Sundays). Thereafter, there was no Sunday service.

The table below lists trains running on at least five days per week. Those on the northern section mostly ran to Nantybwch, except in the early years, while those on the southern part mainly originated at Newport. However, from 1955 until closure, Risca was the termination point for all except the first and last trains each day.

	South of Tredegar	North of Tredegar
1890	3	8
1901	3	9
1910	8	14
1923	10	18
1936	12	17
1948	8	9
1960	4	4

September 1948

Table 120b NANTYBWCH, TREDEGAR, and NEWPORT (Third class only)

Miles	Week Days only	a.m	a.m	a.m		a.m	a.m		p.m	p.m		p.m	p.m	p.m			
	Nantybwch dep	..	6 56	8 17	..	8 50	1110	..	1 50	4 2	..	6 0	..	9 30	..	..	..
1¼	Sirhowy	..	7 1	8 21	..	8 54	1114	..	1 54	4 6	..	6 4	..	9 38	..	..	..
2	**Tredegar** arr	..	7 5	8 25	..	8 58	1118	..	1 58	4 10	..	6 8	..	9 42	..	..	..
	Tredegar dep	5 40	7 6	8 26	..	..	1120	..	1 59	4 12	..	6 10	7 52	9 43	..	..	..
3¾	Bedwellty Pits Halt	5 45	7 11	8 31	..	..	1125	..	2 4	4 17	..	6 15	7 57	9 48	..	..	..
5½	Holly Bush	5 53	7 20	8 39	..	..	1133	..	2 12	4 25	..	6 23	8 5	9 56	..	..	..
6½	Markham Village Halt	5 58	7 24	8 43	..	..	1137	..	2 16	4 29	..	6 27	8 9	10 0	..	..	..
8	Argoed Halt	6 2	7 29	8 47	..	..	1141	..	2 20	4 33	..	6 31	8 13	10 4	..	..	..
9¾	Blackwood	6 9	7 37	8 54	..	..	1149	..	2 27	4 40	..	6 39	8 21	1011	..	..	..
11¼	Pontllanfraith **A** arr	6 14	7 42	8 59	..	..	1154	..	2 32	4 45	..	6 44	8 26	1016	..	..	..
	Pontllanfraith **A** dep	6 15	7 45	9 0	..	..	1155	..	2 34	4 46	..	6 45	8 27	1019	..	..	..
12¼	Wyllie Halt	6 18	7 48	9 3	..	..	1158	..	2 37	4 49	..	6 48	8 30	1022	..	..	..
13¼	Ynysddu	6 21	7 51	9 6	..	..	12 1	..	2 40	4 52	..	6 51	8 33	1025	..	..	..
14¼	Pont Lawrence Halt	6 25	7 55	9 10	..	..	12 5	..	2 44	4 56	..	6 55	8 37	1029	..	..	..
15½	Nine-Mile-Point **B**	6 29	8 1	9 14	..	..	1211	..	2 49	5 0	..	7 1	8 42	1033	..	..	..
18	Risca	6 36	8 8	9 20	..	..	1218	..	2 55	5 6	..	7 7	8 49	..	..	..	..
20¼	Rogerstone	6 42	8 14	..	..	..	1224	..	3 2	..	..	..	8 55	..	..	..	..
21½	Bassaleg Junc. **C**	6 46	8 18	**Aa**	..	..	1228	..	3 6	**Aa**	..	**Aa**	8 59	..	..	..	..
24½	**Newport** arr.	6 53	8 26	9Z46	..	..	1235	..	3 13	5Z31	..	7 25	9 6	..	..	..	..

Miles	Week Days only	a.m	a.m	a.m	a.m	a.m	a.m		p.m	p.m	p.m	p.m		p.m	p.m		
	Newport dep.	4 20	..	..	..	7 22	9 5	..	..	1 10	3 50	5Z40	..	7 37	9 25	..	..
3	Bassaleg Junction **C**	**Kk**	..	..	..	7 29	9 12	..	..	1 17	3 57	5Z47	..	**Kk**	9 37	..	..
4¼	Rogerstone	..	..	..	..	7 33	9 16	..	..	1 21	4 1	..	..	..	9 41	..	..
6½	Risca	4 34	..	..	..	7 39	9 21	..	..	1 26	4 6	6 0	..	7 51	9 46	..	..
9	Nine-Mile-Point **B**	4 40	..	..	..	7 46	9 27	..	..	1 32	4 12	6 5	..	7 57	9 56	..	..
10	Pont Lawrence Halt	..	..	..	..	7 49	9 30	..	..	1 35	4 15	6 8	..	8 0	9 59	..	..
11¼	Ynysddu	4 47	..	..	..	7 54	9 35	..	..	1 40	4 20	6 13	..	8 5	10 4	..	..
12¼	Wyllie Halt	..	..	..	..	7 57	9 38	..	..	1 43	4 23	6 16	..	8 8	10 7	..	..
13¼	Pontllanfraith **A** arr	4 55	..	..	..	8 2	9 43	..	..	1 48	4 28	6 21	..	8 13	1012	..	..
	Pontllanfraith **A** dep	4 57	..	..	..	8 4	9 44	..	..	1 49	4 29	6 22	..	8 14	1013	..	..
14¾	Blackwood	5 4	..	..	..	8 9	9 48	..	..	1 53	4 33	6 27	..	8 18	1018	..	..
16¼	Argoed Halt	..	..	..	..	8 17	9 55	..	..	2 0	4 40	6 34	..	8 26	1025	..	..
18	Markham Village Halt	..	..	..	..	8 22	10 0	..	..	2 5	4 45	6 39	..	8 31	1031	..	..
18¾	Holly Bush	..	..	..	..	8 27	10 5	..	..	2 10	4 50	6 44	..	8 36	1036	..	..
20½	Bedwellty Pits Halt	..	..	..	..	8 34	1012	..	..	2 19	4 57	6 51	..	8 43	1045	..	..
22½	**Tredegar** arr	5 30	..	..	..	8 41	1019	..	..	2 26	5 4	6 58	..	8 50	1052	..	..
	Tredegar dep	..	6 35	6 55	8 2	..	1031	..	1245	2 28	5 5	..	..	8 55	1056	..	..
23¼	Sirhowy	..	6 39	7 5	8 6	..	1035	..	1249	2 32	5 9	..	..	8 58	1059	..	..
24½	**Nantybwch** arr.	..	6 45	7 11	8 12	..	1041	..	1255	2 38	5 15	..	..	9 4	11S6	..	..

A L.M.R. Station; about ¼ mile to W.R. Station
Aa Calls at Bassaleg Junction to set down from Sirhowy Line Stations on notice being given to the Guard
B Station for Upper Machen (1½ miles)
C L.M.R. Station; nearly ½ mile to W.R. Station
Kk Calls when required to take up for Sirhowy Line Stations on notice being given at the Station
S Saturdays only
Z Change at Risca.

November 1959

Table 120 NANTYBWCH, TREDEGAR and NEWPORT

WEEK DAYS ONLY (Second class only)

Miles		am			am			pm			pm			pm			pm E			pm E		
	Nantybwch dep	6 35	..	..	11 0	..	..	..	..	..	4 50	..	..	..	..	..	9 30	..	..	..	..	..
1¼	Sirhowy	6 39	..	..	11 5	..	..	..	..	..	4 54	..	..	..	..	..	9 38	..	..	..	..	..
2	**Tredegar** arr	6 43	..	..	11 10	..	..	..	..	..	4 58	..	..	..	..	..	9 42	..	..	..	..	..
	Tredegar dep	6 44	..	..	11 15	..	..	1 40	..	..	5 0	..	..	7 52	..	..	..	..	..	9 43	..	..
3¾	Bedwellty Pits Halt	6 50	..	..	11 20	..	..	1 45	..	..	5 6	..	..	7 57	..	..	..	..	..	9 48	..	..
5½	Holly Bush	7 0	..	..	11 28	..	..	1 55	..	..	5 14	..	..	8 5	..	..	..	..	..	9 56	..	..
6½	Markham Village Halt	7 5	..	..	11 33	..	..	2 1	..	..	5 18	..	..	8 9	..	..	..	..	..	10 0	..	..
8	Argoed Halt	7 9	..	..	11 37	..	..	2 5	..	..	5 22	..	..	8 13	..	..	..	..	..	10 4	..	..
9¾	Blackwood	7 15	..	..	11 43	..	..	2 11	..	..	5 28	..	..	8 21	..	..	..	..	..	10 11	..	..
11¼	Pontllanfraith **A** arr	7 19	..	..	11 47	..	..	2 16	..	..	5 32	..	..	8 26	..	..	..	..	..	10 16	..	..
	Pontllanfraith **A** dep	7 20	..	..	11 48	..	..	2 17	..	..	5 33	..	..	8 27	..	..	..	..	..	10 19	..	..
12½	Wyllie Halt	7 24	..	..	11 52	..	..	2 21	..	..	5 37	..	..	8 30	..	..	..	..	..	10 22	..	..
13¼	Ynysddu	7 27	..	..	11 55	..	..	2 24	..	..	5 40	..	..	..	..	..	..	..	..	10 25	..	..
18¼	Risca arr	7 40	..	..	12 10	..	..	2 37	..	..	5 53	..	..	8 44	..	..	..	..	..	..	..	..
	Risca dep	7 48	..	..	12 18	..	..	2 41	..	..	6 1	..	..	8 47	..	..	..	..	..	..	..	..
19¼	Tynycwm Halt	7Z50	..	..	12Z21	..	..	2Z43	..	..	6Z 4	..	..	8 49	..	..	..	..	..	..	..	..
20½	Rogerstone	7Z54	..	..	12Z26	..	..	2Z46	..	..	6Z 8	..	..	8 54	..	..	..	..	..	..	..	..
21¾	Bassaleg Junction **D**	7Z58	..	..	12Z29	..	..	2Z50	..	..	6Z11	..	..	8 58	..	..	..	..	..	..	..	..
24½	**Newport** arr	8Z 5	..	..	12 38	..	..	2Z59	..	..	6Z24	..	..	9 6	..	..	..	..	..	..	..	..

Miles		am		am			am		am			pm E		pm		pm S	pm			pm		
	Newport dep	4 20	..	..	..	..	7Z30	..	..	..	..	..	..	12Z 5	..	3Z15	..	..	..	6Z10	..	..
2¾	Bassaleg Junction **D**	**Kk**	..	..	..	..	7Z37	..	..	..	..	..	..	12Z12	..	3Z22	..	..	..	6Z17	..	..
4	Rogerstone	..	..	..	..	..	7Z41	..	..	..	..	..	..	12Z16	..	3Z26	..	..	..	6Z21	..	..
5¼	Tynycwm Halt	..	..	..	..	..	7Z45	..	..	..	..	..	..	12Z20	..	3Z30	..	..	..	6Z25	..	..
6¼	Risca arr	4 34	..	..	..	..	7 47	..	..	..	..	..	..	12 23	..	3 33	..	..	..	6 27	..	..
	Risca dep	4 35	..	..	..	..	7 55	..	..	..	..	..	..	12 30	..	3 36	..	..	..	6 32	..	..
11¼	Ynysddu	4 47	..	..	..	..	8 7	..	..	..	..	..	..	12 43	..	3 48	..	..	..	6 44	..	..
12¼	Wyllie Halt	..	..	..	..	..	8 10	..	..	..	..	..	..	12 45	..	3 51	..	..	..	6 47	..	..
13¼	Pontllanfraith **A** arr	4 55	..	..	..	..	8 15	..	..	..	..	..	..	12 50	..	3 55	..	..	..	6 52	..	..
	Pontllanfraith **A** dep	4 57	..	..	..	..	8 16	..	..	..	..	..	..	12 51	..	3 56	..	..	..	6 53	..	..
14¾	Blackwood	5 4	..	..	..	..	8 20	..	..	..	..	..	..	12 55	..	4 0	..	..	..	6 57	..	..
16½	Argoed Halt	..	..	..	..	..	8 26	..	..	..	..	..	..	1 1	..	4 7	..	..	..	7 3	..	..
18	Markham Village Halt	..	..	..	..	..	8 31	..	..	..	..	..	..	1 6	..	4 12	..	..	..	7 8	..	..
18¾	Holly Bush	..	..	..	..	..	8 35	..	..	..	..	..	..	1 10	..	4 16	..	..	..	7 13	..	..
20¼	Bedwellty Pits Halt	..	..	..	..	..	8 44	..	..	..	..	..	..	1 18	..	4 23	..	..	..	7 20	..	..
22½	**Tredegar** arr	5 40	..	..	..	..	8 50	..	..	..	..	..	..	1 25	..	4 30	..	..	..	7 27	..	..
	Tredegar dep	..	..	6 20	..	..	..	..	1025	..	..	1255	..	..	..	..	4 32	..	..	..	..	..
23¼	Sirhowy	..	..	6 23	..	..	..	..	1030	..	..	1259	..	..	..	..	4 36	..	..	..	..	..
24½	**Nantybwch** arr	..	..	6 28	..	..	..	..	1037	..	..	1 5	..	..	..	..	4 42	..	..	..	..	..

A High Level; about ¼ mile to Low Level
D Nearly ¼ mile to Bassaleg Station
E or E Except Saturdays

Kk Calls when required to take up for Ynysddu and beyond on notice being given at Bassaleg Jn.
S Saturdays only

Z Change at Risca

June 1969

November 1930

NANTYBWCH, SIRHOWY, TREDEGAR. and NEWPORT.—Sirhowy.

Gen. Man., R. Bond.]   **Sundays.**

				Sundays.				Newport dep									
Nantybwch dp		8 59	55	2 25	6 25				9 15	2 30	6 50		6 0			
Sirhowy	7 45	8 14	10 11	236	2 41	4 50 6 31 8 18	8 25	11 25	4 107 25	Risca (Dock St	9 35	2 50	7 0	10 20	6 20	
Tredegar arr	7 48	8 20	10 5	238	2 45	4 54 6 35 8 22	8 28	11 30	4 17 30	Nine-Mile-P	9 45	3 0	7 2	1030	6 30	
dep	7 50		1240		4 56	8 30	4 15			Tredegar J. a	9 57				6 43	
Argoed	8 7		1258		5 13	8 46	4 31			26, 27 d	10 7	3 15	7 35	1045	6 45	
Blackwood	8 13		1 5		5 19	8 54	4 37			Blackwood	1012	3 20	7 43	1053	6 53	
Tredegar J.			5 24			9 0	4 42			Argoed	1018	3 27	7 49	1059	6 59	
26, 27	8 18		1 10		5 28	9 0	4 42			Tredegar a	1037		8 8			
Nine-Mile-Pn	8 30		1 25		5 45	9 15	4 55			d	6 45	7 35	8 40	1040	1 20	3 46 5 15	8 15	1117 4 0 7 17
Risca 30, 30, 120	8 40		1 33		5 53	9 23	5 4			Sirhowy	6 49	7 40	7 46	9 45	1044	1 20 3 50 5 10	8 14	8 20 1120 4 5 7 20
Nwprt 28, 29, 8	9 0		1 55		6 15	9 45	5 30			Nantybwch a	6 55	7 55	9 50	1 25	5 15	

Tuesdays only. / Tuesdays only. / Thursdays. / Sundays.

A All 1, 2, 3 class. The Trains do not stop between Risca and Newport, and Quarry Mawr.

NANTYBWCH, TREDEGAR, and NEWPORT.—London and North Western.

Down.   Week Days.

Miles		mrn	mrn	mrn	mrn	mrn	mrn	mrn	aft	aft	aft	aft		aft	aft		aft	aft	
—	Nantybwch dep		7 22	8 35	8 45	1017	1110	2	5 2	4 36	6 15			8 25		10 5	
1¼	Sirhowy		7 27	8 40	8 50	1022	1115	2	5 2	4 7	4 40	6 20			8 30		1010	
2	Tredegar arr	6 10	7 30	8 44	8 54	1025	1110	2	9 3	0 4	4 46	6 24					1014	
	dep	6 10	7 31	8 45		1027		1130	2 10		4 49	6 30		8 20		9 50	
4½	Bedwellty Pits	6 15	7 35	8 49		1031		1134	2 14		4 54	6 34		8 25		9 54	
5½	Holly Bush	6 20	7 39	8 53		1036		1139	2 19		5 0	6 40		8 31		9 59	
8	Argoed	6 25	7 44	8 58		1041		12 4	2 24		5 5	6 44		8 41		10 4	
10½	Blackwood	6 30	7 48	9 2		1046		12 9	2 29		5 10	6 50		8 57		10 9	
11½	Tredegar Junction arr	6 36	7 52	9 6		1051		1214	2 34		5 15	6 55		5 57		1014	
	dep	6 37	7 52	9 6		1052		1215	2 35		5 25	6 56		8 41		1015	
13½	Ynysddu	6 42	7 56	9 11		1057		1220	2 40		5 27	1		9 4		1020	
15½	Nine-Mile-Point	6 47	8 1	9 16		11 3		1226	2 45		5 41	7 6		9 10		1026	
18	Risca 70		8 10	9 26		1112		1235	2 55		5 50	7 15		9 20		1035	
22½	Bassaleg 463	68	a	a		a		a	a		a	a		a		a	
24½	Newport + 58 to 65.		8 25	9 41		1127		1250	3 10		6 5	7 30		9 35		1050	

Up.

Mls		mrn	mrn	mrn	mrn	mrn	aft	aft	aft		aft	aft	aft		aft		aft	
—	Newport (High St.) dep			8 45		10 5	1217	2	2 0	4		6 55	9 28		1030		1123	
2	Bassaleg			8 55		b			b	b		b	b					
6½	Risca			9 2		1022	1234	2	2 47	4 27		7 12	9 45				1144	
9	Nine-Mile-Point		8 10	9 9		1029	1243	2	2 56	4 34		7 19	9 52		1052		1144	
11½	Ynysddu		8 15	9 15		1035	1249	3	3 4	40		7 25	9 57		108		1151	
13½	Tredegar Junction arr		8 20	9 19		1040	1254	3	3 9	4 46		7 31	10 2		114		1156	
	dep		8 29	9 23		1041	1255	3	3 14	4 52		7 41	10 9		1114		1157	
14½	Blackwood		8 27	9 32		1046	1 0	3	3 16	4 55		7 46	10 8		1114		
16½	Argoed		8 33	9 37		1052	1 6	3	3 22	5 1		7 52	1014		1115		1210	
18½	Holly Bush		8 39	9 43		1058	1 13	3	3 29	5 4		7 58	1020		1120		1213	
20½	Bedwellty Pits		8 45	9 48		11 3	1 19	3	3 35	5 10		8 4	1025		1125		1220	
22½	Tredegar arr		8 50	9 52		11 7	1 24	3	3 40	5 15		8 9	1030		1130		1224	
	dep	6 50	8 50	9 50	30 9	53	1040		1 30	2 55	4		5 45	8 27	1035		1130		1225	
23½	Sirhowy	6 55	8 19	9 35	10 0	1045		1 35	2 50	2 57	3 45	4 25	5 27	8 14	9 40	1035		1136		1229	
24½	Nantybwch 464 arr	7 0	8 24	9 40	10 5	1050		11 40	2 55	3 25	3 55	3 77	100		9 45	

a Stops to set down from Sirhowy Line on notice being given to the Guard.
b Stops to take up for Sirhowy Line on notice being given at the Station.
c Calls at Pochin Pits Colliery Platform on Saturdays.
* Station for Upper Machen (1½ miles).
+ High St. Station.

Saturdays only. / Mondays Thursdays & Saturdays. / Mondays Wednesdays & Thursdays. / Saturdays only. / Mondays & Thursdays.

NANTYBWCH, TREDEGAR, and NEWPORT.—L. M. & S. and G. W.

Down.   Week Days only.

Miles		mrn	mrn	mrn	mrn	mrn	mrn	aft	aft	aft	S	E	aft	aft		S	E	E	S	S
—	Nantybwch dep	7 12	8 22	8 50	9 23	9 38	1035	1115	5 1	5 53	0			5 15	5 45	6 30	7 35	8 50	9 30	1010	1010	1051
1½	Sirhowy	7 17	8 28	8 55	9 28	9 43	1040	1121	5 1	02	0 37			5 19	5 50	6 37	7 41	8 59	9 35	1015	1015	1057
2	Tredegar arr	7 20	8 32	9 0	9 31	9 46	1043	1124	13 2	9 30				5 30	5 36	6 47	7 48	8 33	18 9	43	1018	1018	11 0
	dep	5 50	7 22	8 34		9 53		1130	1 20	2 13	4 10	4 50	4 55	5 58	7 52	9 29	9 45	1022
3½	Bedwellty Pits	5 55	7 26	8 39		9 58		1135	1 26	2 17	4 14	4 54		6 3	7 57	9 30	9 50	1027
4½	Holly Bush	6 0	7 31	8 44		10 6		1140	1 31	2 22	4 19	5 0		6 8	8 3	9 40	10 0	1032
6½	Markham Village Halt	6 9	7 34	8 47		10 6		1144	1 35	2 25	4 23	5 4		6 11	8 7	9 40	10 0	1037
8	Argoed	6 14	7 38	8 51		1011		1149	1 39	2 30	4 27	5 85	9	6 16	8 12	9 46	10 6	1043
9½	Blackwood	6 20	7 44	8 56		1017		1156	1 45	2 36	4 33	5 14	5 18	5 18	8 22	9 56	1016	1053
11	Pontllanfraith A 82	6 24	7 49	9 0		1021		12 0	1 49	2 40	4 37	5 18	5 26	8 22	9 56	1016	1059
	34 dep	6 26	7 50	9 2		1022		12 1	1 50	2 43	4 39	5 19	5 19	8 18	5 20	10 0	1055
12½	Ynysddu	6 31	7 55	9 7		1027		12 6	1 55	2 48	4 44	5 24	5 24	6 34	8 26	10 4	1025	11 0
14	Pont Lawrence	6 34	7 59	9 10		1031		1210	1 58	2 52	4 47	5 27		6 38	8 32	10 9	1038	11 4
15½	Nine-Mile-Point B	6 39	8 4	9 15		1036		1216	2 3	2 57	4 52	5 32		6 43	8 37	1014	1031	11 6
18	Risca 81	6 44	8 10	9 20		1041		1221	2 8	3 4	4 58	5 18	5 37	33	4 48	8 42	1019	
22½	Bassaleg Junc. C 87b		504	Aa	Aa	Aa								5 29	Aa		Aa	Aa	Aa	
24½	Newport D 62, 67, 78, arr.	7 0	8 27	9 37		1058		1237	2 23	3 19	5 15			5 59	9 0	1037

Up.   Week Days only.

Miles		mrn	mrn	mrn	mrn	mrn	mrn	mrn	aft	aft	aft	aft	aft	S	E	S
—	Newport (High Street) dep	4 30			7 22	8 50		1038	E	S	1210	103 10	4	8 4 57		7 35	9 59	55	1039	1110
3	Bassaleg Junction C					Bb		Bb			Bb	Bb	Bb				
6½	Risca	4 47			7 409	5		1053			1226	1 263	26	4 245	155	7 52	9 22	1013	1053	1126
9	Nine-Mile-Point B	4 54			7 479	11		11 0			1231	323	32	4 255	20	7 57	9 29	1020	1059	1132
10	Pont Lawrence				7 519	14		11 4			1237	338	38	4 33		9 0	9 33	1024	11 2	1136
11½	Ynysddu				7 569	18		1111			1242	393	393	44	4 43		5 34	9 5	9 37	1028	11 6	1140
13½	Pontllanfraith A 82, arr	5 6			8 1	9 23		1116			1247	443	45	4 43	5 39	8 10	9 41	1033	1112	1145
	34 dep	5 9			8 9	9 25		1120			1250	463	46	4 45		5 51	8 18	9 50	1041	1117	1152
14½	Blackwood	5 16			8 18	9 31		1126			1256	1 533	52	4 45		5 46	8 18	9 51	1046	1123	1157
16½	Argoed	5 22			8 23	9 36		1131			1 1	1 583	58	5 0		5 51	8 25	10 6	1055	1136	12 4
18½	Markham Village Halt				8 32	9 44		1138			1 102	6	4 4	6	5 5		6 0	8 37	1010	11 0	1140
19½	Holly Bush	5 31			8 37	9 48		1143			1 142	10 4	10	5 9		6 5	8 37	1010 11	0 1140
20½	Bedwellty Pits				8 42	9 53		1148			1 192	16	16	5 19		6 10	8 42	1018 11	12 1150
22½	Tredegar arr	5 39			8 47	9 58		1153			1 242	204	20	5 19	45 26		6 14	8 47	1024 1112	1150 1221
	dep	6 50	8 50	8 28	9 13	1016	1053		12 5	1215	1 35	225		4 335	266	87 18	8 8 53	9 35	1033 1120	1156 1220
23½	Sirhowy	6 53	8 58	8 28	9 19	1016	1053		12 8	1218	1 38	228	28	4 405	346	157 25	8 58	9 40	1040
24½	Nantybwch 484 arr	7 1	8 10	8 40	9 20	1023	11 0		12 15	1225	1 452	36	4 405	346	157 25	8 17	9 5	9 47	1040

NOTES.

A About ¼ mile to G.W. Station.
Aa Calls at Bassaleg Junction to set down from Sirhowy Line Station on notice being given to the Guard.
B Station for Upper Machen (1½ miles).
Bb Calls at Bassaleg Junction when required to take up for Sirhowy Line Station on notice being given at the Station.
C Nearly ¼ mile to G. W. (late B. & M.) Sta.
D High Street.
E Except Saturdays.
S Saturdays only.

Dep. Abergavenny J'n at 9 50 mrn, see page 484. / Dep. Abergavenny J'n. at 8 30 mrn, see page 484. / Arr. Abergavenny Jn. 9 25 mrn, see page 484.

SIRHOWY TRAMROAD

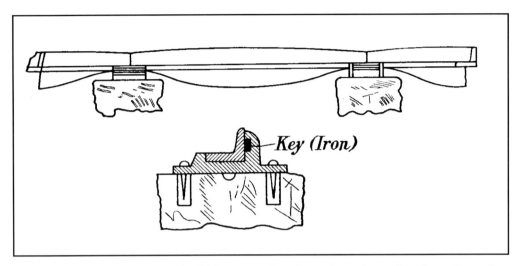

Key (Iron)

1.   The line reached a length of 24 miles and used cast iron plates of angle configuration, with fish-belly undersides. The plates were 3ft long and laid to a gauge of 4ft 2ins on stone blocks, until 1840.

2.   Between about 1840 and 1860, the tramway employed wrought iron rails in chairs, fixed to timber sleepers. Despite a 4mph speed limit, there were many breakages. Contractors paid for access to the track.

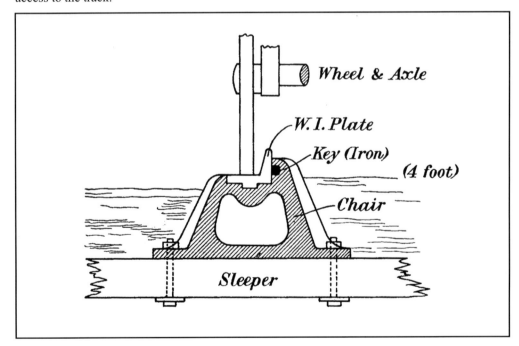

Wheel & Axle

W. I. Plate

Key (Iron)

(4 foot)

Chair

Sleeper

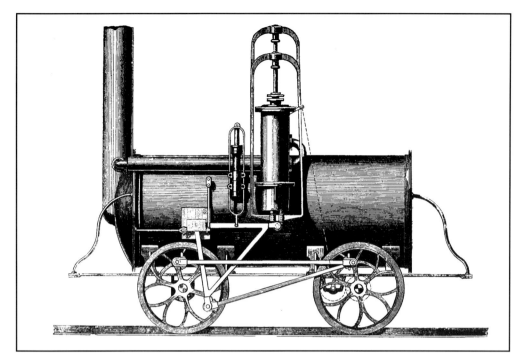

3.   *Speedwell* was built in 1830 by the Neath Abbey Iron Works and it is shown to have a feed water heater around the exhaust pipe. Little is known of *Hercules*, which came from the same firm in 1829. It seems that both belonged to Thomas Prothero of Newport.

4.   *St. David* was built by the Tredegar Iron Company in about 1830-32 for its own traffic. It was designed by its engineer, Thomas Ellis, and extensively rebuilt in 1848. The LNWR took over a stock of nine standard gauge locomotives in 1876; most had been built by the Vulcan Foundry.

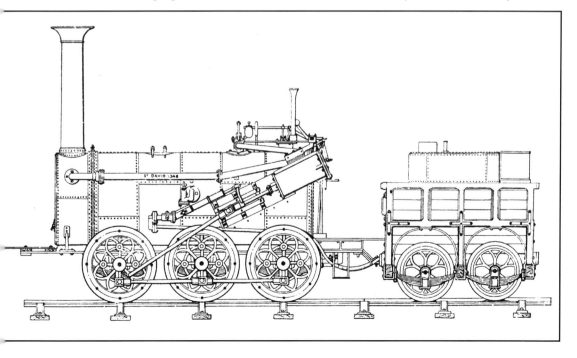

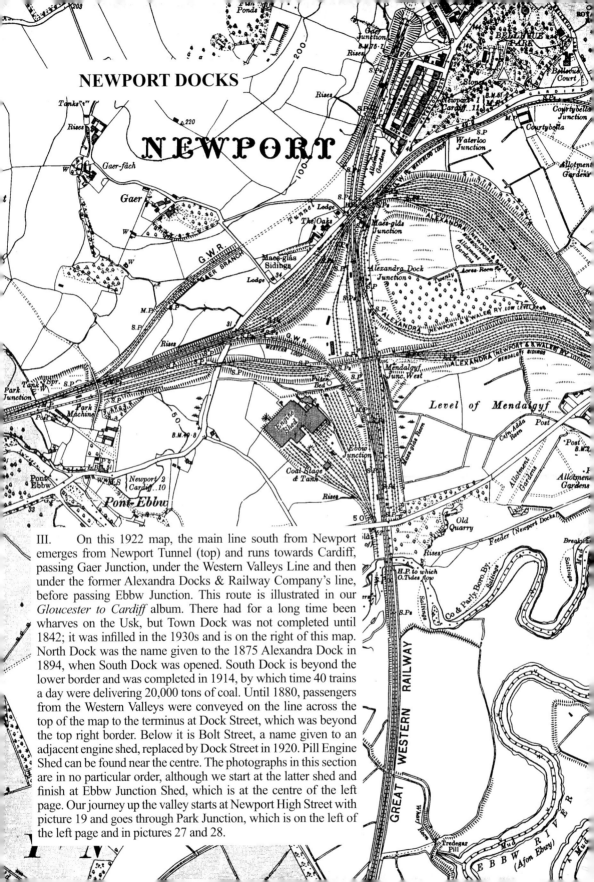

NEWPORT DOCKS

NEWPORT

III.　　On this 1922 map, the main line south from Newport emerges from Newport Tunnel (top) and runs towards Cardiff, passing Gaer Junction, under the Western Valleys Line and then under the former Alexandra Docks & Railway Company's line, before passing Ebbw Junction. This route is illustrated in our *Gloucester to Cardiff* album. There had for a long time been wharves on the Usk, but Town Dock was not completed until 1842; it was infilled in the 1930s and is on the right of this map. North Dock was the name given to the 1875 Alexandra Dock in 1894, when South Dock was opened. South Dock is beyond the lower border and was completed in 1914, by which time 40 trains a day were delivering 20,000 tons of coal. Until 1880, passengers from the Western Valleys were conveyed on the line across the top of the map to the terminus at Dock Street, which was beyond the top right border. Below it is Bolt Street, a name given to an adjacent engine shed, replaced by Dock Street in 1920. Pill Engine Shed can be found near the centre. The photographs in this section are in no particular order, although we start at the latter shed and finish at Ebbw Junction Shed, which is at the centre of the left page. Our journey up the valley starts at Newport High Street with picture 19 and goes through Park Junction, which is on the left of the left page and in pictures 27 and 28.

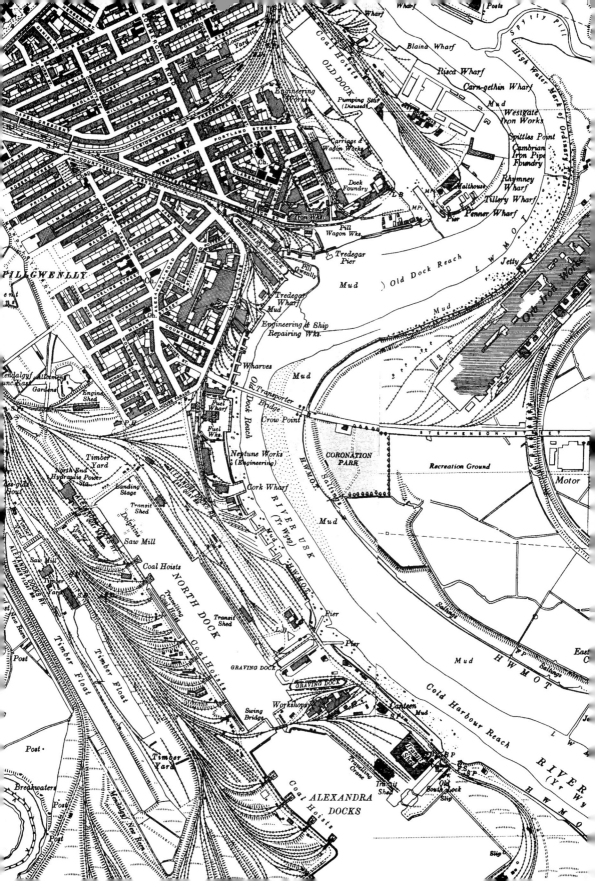

5.   This is an eastward view of Pill Shed in September 1963 and it has the combined water tank and coal stage on the right. In the background is the unusual Transporter Bridge, which is marked on the centre of the right page of the map. (R.S.Carpenter)

6.   Standing alongside the shed on 19th June 1949 is GWR no. 667. It was ex-ADR and still had a wooden buffer beam. This company built its engine shed on the site and the GWR rebuilt it in 1929. It closed in 1963, when its code was 86B, by which time the remaining dock shunting work had been dieselised. (T.J.Edgington)

7.   The Monmouthshire Sidings are seen from the south, with the bridge over the main line in the left background. This group of sidings are top right on the left page of the map and were known as "Mon Bank". (Steam)

8.   A panorama of North Dock in 1927 features some of the countless telegraph poles which were imported in that decade. There was a creosoting plant nearby, operated by Burt Boltons. (Steam)

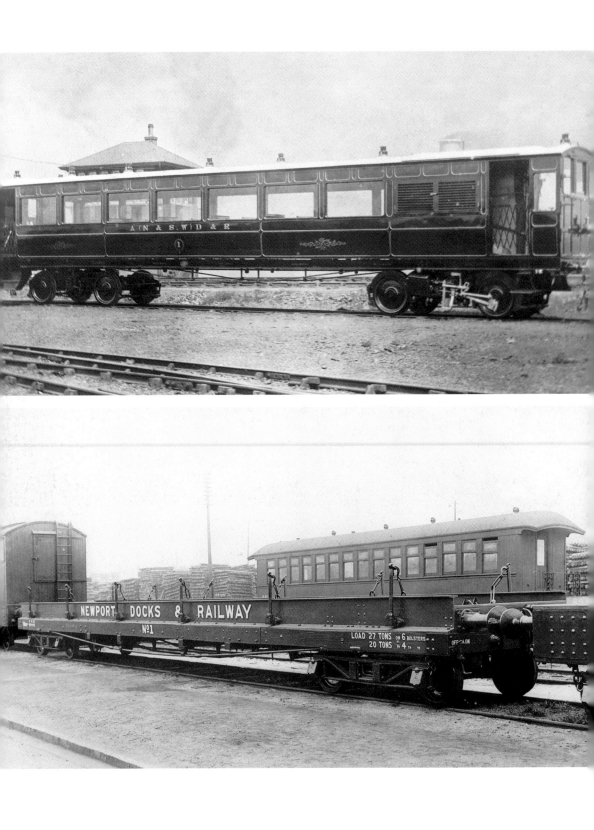

←——— 9.   This steam railmotor carries the initials of the Alexandra (Newport & South Wales) Docks & Railway, ADR in brief. Two were received from the Glasgow Railway and Engineering Co. Ltd in 1904-05 and often worked between Caerphilly and Pontypridd. One lasted until 1911 and the other to 1917. (R.Caston coll.)

←——— 10.   Barnum & Bailey's circus came from the USA to tour much of Britain in the years around 1900 and they brought their own rolling stock. Some items were acquired by the ADR, such as this wagon and the performers coach behind. (R.Caston coll.)

11.   A special train of Admiralty buoys was recorded on 22nd April 1934. They are on the sidings seen in the other direction in picture 7. (R.Caston coll.)

12.   An incoming shipment of potatoes is seen at North Dock in the 1930s. Electric cranes were introduced in 1927, but much labour was still required at each end of their arc. Some of the vast quantities of coal wagons to and from the hoists can be seen in the background. (R.Caston coll.)

→ 13.   Many coal hoists are shown on the map and here is a small selection of them at Alexandra Docks. Loading figures of around 20,000 tons per day were often recorded. (R.Caston coll.)

More aspects of Newport Docks can
be seen in pictures 1-25 in our
Monmouthshire Eastern Valleys volume.

14.   Grabs are being used to unload imported iron ore in March 1954. The 0-6-0T is ex-ADR no. 666 and the travelling cranes are by Stothert & Pitt of Bath. There was still considerable traffic at the docks in 2007, notably class 66 diesel locomotives imported from the USA. Bulk traffics include imported coal, also exported steel and scrap metals. (R.Caston coll.)

15.   Over 800 2-8-0s came from the USA prior to the invasion of France in 1944 and many were stored and prepared at Ebbw Junction Shed. This view is from the roof of the repair shop, featured in the next picture. The US Army had received 104 2-8-0s at Newport by 7th September 1943 and, by 17th May 1944, a further 358 had arrived, plus 70 0-6-0Ts and 24 diesels. Around 300 servicemen were involved in commissioning these, plus erecting 251 40-ton "cistern cars". (World War Two Railway Study Group)

16.   The building was also known as the fitting shop, the lifting shop and the factory. It is seen on 22nd September 1962, with the running sheds on the left. Each had a central 65ft turntable from which 28 lines radiated. The depot was in use from July 1915 until October 1965. A diesel depot was established on the right in 1966 and can be seen in picture 102 in *Gloucester to Cardiff*. (R.S.Carpenter)

17.　　The traverser in the foreground gave access to the nine roads of the repair shop. Waiting their turn in about 1953 are nos 436 (ex-B&MR), 4130 and 5229. The table was electrically propelled, but lighting was by gas. There was an allocation of around 130 locomotives here in the 1950s. (R.S.Carpenter)

18.　　This southward panorama over the site of the former Alexandra Dock Junction West is from 27th August 1998 and has the Alexandra Docks lines curving to the left. Nos 37673 and 37674 are working the 14.50 EWS Enterprise service to St. Blazey, in Cornwall. Only parts of the South Dock lines were in use, mainly for coal and steel. (B.Morrison)

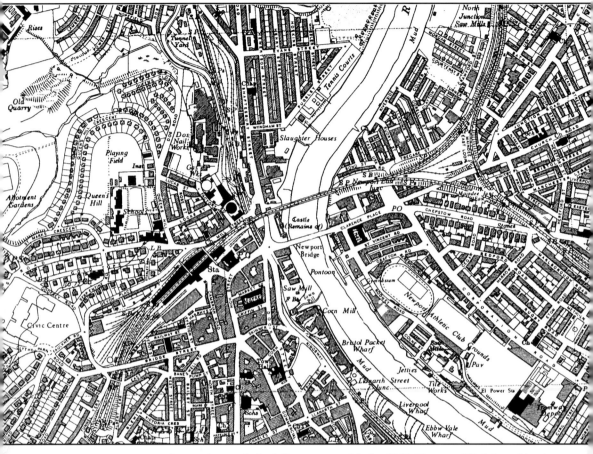

IV.   We start our journey here, as indeed all passengers did after 1880. The term "High Street" has been used intermittently. The 1947 map at 6 ins to 1 mile has the line from Swindon on the right, Hereford top right and our route enters the tunnels lower left. The sidings west of the station lasted until 2006.

19.   Poor visibility prevailed here, due to cuttings and tunnels at the west end, where there had been an engine shed until 1915. These are the two northern platforms in 1930 and they were

used mainly by Valley trains. The island platform (left) has seen most traffic since 1962, but in 2007 work began on extending the one on the right. Becoming No. 4, it was provided with a new canopy and new entrance buildings were planned. (Mowat coll./ Brunel University)

20.   A prestigious new building was erected on the south side and it was photographed on 29th October 1929. The wooden scaffold poles were tied together with ropes. (GWR)

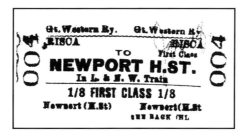

21.   Ex-LMS 0-6-2T no. 7752 heads a two-coach train for Nantybwch on 19th August 1950. Electrically operated points and semaphore signals were in use here from 1927 to 1962. (M.Whitehouse coll.)

Gt Western Ry   Gt Western Ry
2623   RISCA   RISCA
                  TO   S.80
NEWPORT H.ST
THIRD CLASS
10d Fare 10d
Issued subject to the conditions&regulations set out in the Company's Time Tables Bills&Notices
Newport H.St   Newport H.St
2623

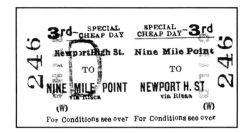

246   **3rd** SPECIAL   SPECIAL **3rd**
              CHEAP DAY   CHEAP DAY
Newport High St.   Nine Mile Point
         TO   TO
NINE MILE POINT   **NEWPORT H.ST**
via Risca   via Risca
(W)   (W)
For Conditions see over   For Conditions see over
246

22.   An eastward panorama in 1964 features a down main line train at the island platform and a "Warship" diesel on a siding that once led to the engine shed, which opened in 1854. It had been the base for 114 locomotives in January 1901. The lines on the right run to the 1926 goods shed, which could house 47 railway wagons and 120 carts. It closed in 1972. (Stations UK)

23.   There had been separate bridges for passengers and parcels, but the former was replaced by a subway in November 1977. However, the gates are closed as it was, and still is, used as a public thoroughfare, passengers using the remaining bridge. This and the next picture are dated 29th May 1986. (C.G.Maggs)

24.   The rebuilding in 1875-80 resulted in this elegant structure and the vaulted roof design gave uniform natural lighting. The complex subject of platform renumbering is addressed in our other albums, as is resignalling. (C.G.Maggs)

25.   In the background of this westward view from 30th May 2001 are the Godfrey Road locomotives stabling sidings. These were closed on 27th May 2006. The Pacer unit is carrying the Valley Lines logo and such stock may run to Ebbw Vale again from here, although the reopening plan envisaged Cardiff as the destination, initially. (M.Turvey)

Other views of this station can be found in:

Brecon to Newport
Gloucester to Cardiff
Hereford to Newport
Monmouthshire Eastern Valleys
Swindon to Newport

WEST OF NEWPORT

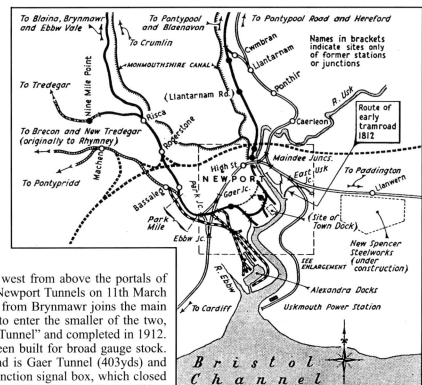

To Blaina, Brynmawr and Ebbw Vale

To Pontypool and Blaenavon

To Pontypool Road and Hereford

To Crumlin

Cwmbran

Llantarnam

Names in brackets indicate sites only of former stations or junctions

MONMOUTHSHIRE CANAL

Ponthir

To Tredegar

Nine Mile Point

(Llantarnam Rd.)

R. Usk

Risca

Rogerstone

Caerleon

Route of early tramroad 1812

To Brecon and New Tredegar (originally to Rhymney)

Machen

Maindee Juncs.

High St

Usk

To Paddington

NEWPORT

East Jc.

Llanwern

To Pontypridd

Bassaleg

Park Jc.

Gaer Jc.

(Site of Town Dock)

New Spencer Steelworks (under construction)

Park Mile

Ebbw Jc.

SEE ENLARGEMENT

R. Ebbw

Alexandra Docks

To Cardiff

Uskmouth Power Station

Bristol Channel

V. Our route is on the left, marked "To Tredegar" and High Street station is near the centre. (Railway Magazine 1960)

26.   We look west from above the portals of the 742yd long Newport Tunnels on 11th March 1959 as a DMU from Brynmawr joins the main line. It is about to enter the smaller of the two, known as "New Tunnel" and completed in 1912. The other had been built for broad gauge stock. In the background is Gaer Tunnel (403yds) and centre is Gaer Junction signal box, which closed on 27th November 1961. (S.Rickard/J&J coll.)

27.   Park Junction is seen from the east on 13th September 1956, the train on the right being bound for Newport from one of the Western Valleys. The engine on the left has come from Ebbw Junction. The straight tracks connect with Newport Docks, which are to the left. (S.Rickard/J&J coll.)

28.   The same signal box is seen in 1986. There had been two parallel single lines northwards from here to Bassaleg since 1981, plus one reversible line (centre) serving the docks. There had earlier been six tracks north hereof; see the next map, lower right. However, the centre line became a siding and the route to Gaer Junction became single; it is lower right. (D.K.Jones coll.)

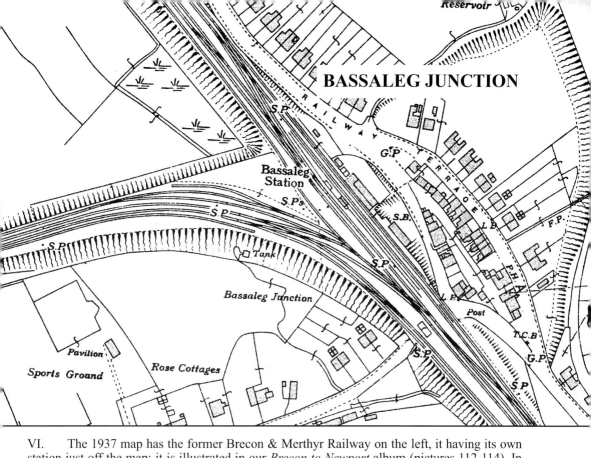

BASSALEG JUNCTION

Reservoir

Bassaleg
Station

Bassaleg Junction

Tank

Pavilion

Sports Ground

Rose Cottages

Post

VI.   The 1937 map has the former Brecon & Merthyr Railway on the left, it having its own station just off the map; it is illustrated in our *Brecon to Newport* album (pictures 112-114). In 2007, this route had a single line to Machen for stone traffic and the single line northwards to Ebbw Vale had been idle since 2001; it awaited reopening to passengers.

29.   The line south of Park Junction was known as "Park Mile" or the "Golden Mile" and was subject to a toll by the local landowner until 1923. It has just been traversed by 0-6-2T no. 5657, which is bound for Blaina on 30th July 1960. The massive 95-lever signal box was in use from 1899 until 1968. (M.Hale)

30. A northward view in about 1969 has the remaining tracks in the distance and on the left are the cooling towers of Rogerstone Power Station. The station building was in commercial use at this time. It has since been demolished and housing occupies the site.
(Lens of Sutton coll.)

NORTH OF BASSALEG JUNCTION

31. No. 37241 runs north on 22nd October 1982 with empties destined for Marine Colliery. A new station was proposed near the site of the power station sidings, one mile north of this wooded area. (T.Heavyside)

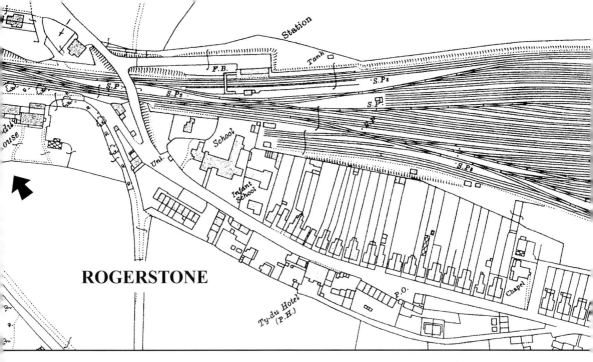

ROGERSTONE

VII.   The first station here was called Tydu and it opened in 1851. It was named Rogerstone from 1898 and in 1900 quadruple track and a new station were provided. The marshalling yard was started in 1885 and passenger lines were laid north of it in 1900, as shown on this 1920 map.

32.   This southward panorama from the road bridge is from between December 1929, when the passenger lines were moved again, further north of the marshalling yard, and June 1931, when the hump was added to the yard to allow gravitational shunting of loaded down trains. The western group of sidings was used for the sorting of empty wagons returning to the valleys. (R.Caston coll.)

33.   The building on the right of the previous picture is seen here, but with a signal box having been added on top of it. However, it did not function as such, but was the Hump Control cabin; it was in use until 28th November 1966, when the yard closed. (Lens of Sutton coll.)

Further photographs and details of the signal boxes in the region of this station and also Bassaleg Junction can be found in *Abertillery and Ebbw Vale Lines.*

TYNYCWM HALT

34.   An island platform was provided on the passenger lines from 17th April 1935 until withdrawal of service from the Western Valleys line on 30th April 1962. Double track from this vicinity to a point north of Cross Keys was required again for the new passenger service. Tickets were issued from the hut attached to the footbridge. The letter survives to carry a public footpath. (M.Hale)

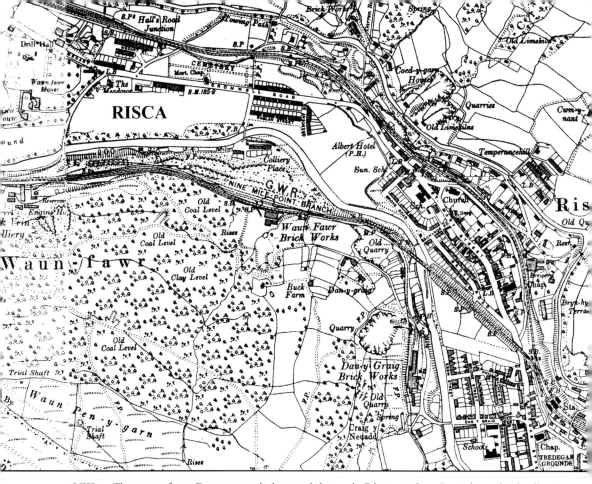

VIII.   The route from Rogerstone is lower right, as is Risca station. Just above it, the line to Sirhowy diverges left from the Ebbw Vale line. The undeveloped quadrangle of land west of the junction was occupied by the Sirhowy Tramway, the route passing over the river and joining the alignment of the brickworks siding shown on this 1922 map, which is at 6 ins to 1 mile.

35.   A westward view across the valley in 1900 from the road above the station features the tramway viaduct. It had partially collapsed. (Railway Magazine)

36.   The station was rebuilt with four platforms in 1910, following the quadrupling of the
route from Pontymister North Sidings box, which is lower right on the next map.
(Lens of Sutton coll.)

37.   A southward view at the north end of the siding leading to Dan-y-Graig Brickworks
shows the alignment of the Sirhowy Tramway and the building thought to house its horses and
staff. The photograph is from the late 1930s; the building is on the right of picture no. 35. The
siding closed on 1st February 1965. (D.S.Barrie)

38.   The junction and signal box are almost hidden in this indifferent postcard view of the sharp curvature; this was dictated by the topography. (Lens of Sutton coll.)

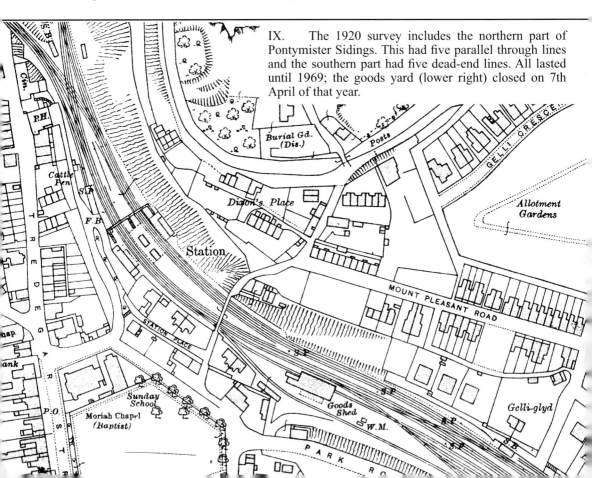

IX.   The 1920 survey includes the northern part of Pontymister Sidings. This had five parallel through lines and the southern part had five dead-end lines. All lasted until 1969; the goods yard (lower right) closed on 7th April of that year.

39.   Standing on the up main, bound for the Sirhowy branch, is Aberbeeg-based 2-8-0T no. 5249 in 1959. Four diamond crossings are in view. (D.K.Jones coll.)

40.   An autocoach is propelled towards the end of its journey at Risca from Nantybwch, sometime in 1959. The Sirhowy line was operated in this manner from June 1954 to its end in 1960. The train is about to pass the 57-lever Risca Junction signal box, which was in use until 22nd December 1968. (M.J.Stretton coll.)

41.   The last train of the day (7.52pm from Tredegar) was the only one not to terminate here. It was hauled by 0-6-0PT no. 9644 on 7th May 1960 and also carried mail. (R.E.Toop)

42.   No. 3634 worked on the last day of service, 11th June 1960 and is standing at the branch platform, waiting to leave with the 3.36pm (Saturdays only) to Nantybwch. (E.Wilmshurst)

43.   The last train to run the entire length of the valley on 11th June 1960 was the 4.50pm from Nantybwch. The 0-6-0PT was noted as no. 8711. There was a 7.52 down from Tredegar, which could make the same claim. The other trains that day also ran through between Risca and Nantybwch. The rails remained shiny, as coal traffic continued on the Sirhowy line until 1970 and steel was conveyed on the Ebbw Vale route until 2001. The junction was at Rogerstone North between 1968 and 1970. (D.K.Jones coll.)

Our *Abertillery and Ebbw Vale Lines* album contains other views of Risca in pictures 11 to 14.

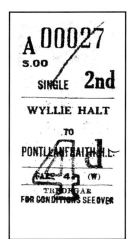

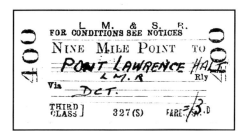

WEST OF RISCA

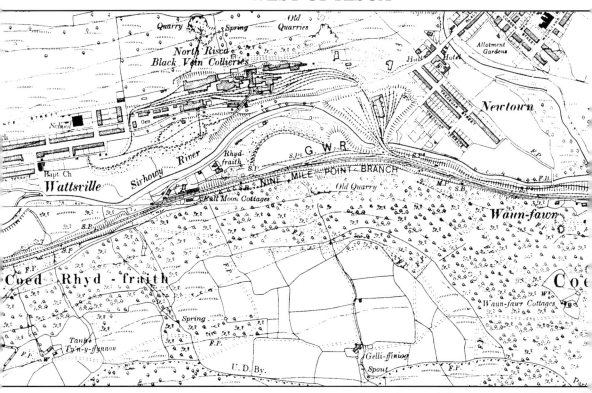

X.   Waun-fawr is shown on this map, but its brickworks is on no. VIII. Its siding was in use from 1910 to 1956. The pronunciation is usually "Wine Vower". The colliery lines shown here mostly survived until about 1950.

XI.   The original Black Vein Colliery is on no. X. The sidings were in use by 1868 and lasted until about 1935. This extract is from 1920.

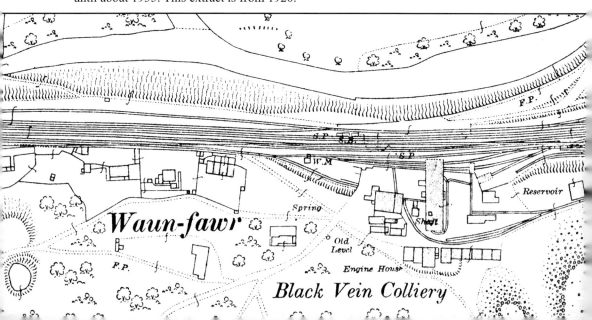

NINE MILE POINT

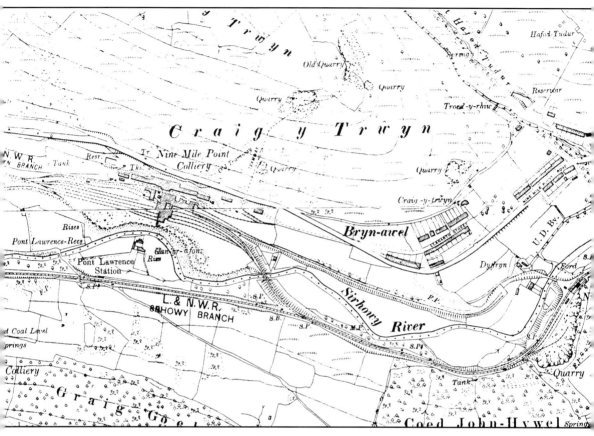

XII.   The Penllwyn Tramway used the curved embankment and narrow bridge shown top left on this 1920 map at 6ins to 1 mile. It had been relaid with conventional track by the LNWR in 1904, but by 1908, the new bridge and connection in the centre of the map was ready. The earlier track remained as a siding, with access from the west only, as shown. It served as Wattsville Goods Depot from 1913 until 2nd August 1929. On the left is Pont Lawrence station.

44.   This is a westward view of the junction shown in the middle of the map above. The box was known as Nine Mile Point No. 1 and its 25-lever frame was in use until 20th November 1967. The branch was not used after 11th March 1969. (D.S.Barrie)

45.   Another photograph from the 1930s and this includes the staggered platforms of one of the oddest named stations. The nine miles was from Court-y-Bella zero post in Newport. In the background near the watertank can just be discerned the GWR Nine Mile Point signal box, which closed in December 1935, but was retained for its telephone links. (D.S.Barrie)

XIII.   The 1920 survey shows the route of the Penllwyn Tramway in use as a roadway between the station and the two sidings of Wattsville Goods Yard. The boundary between the LNWR and the GWR is above the word "Nine", the signal box being GWR property. The lower siding was for the Pennant Stone Quarry and was in use until 1939. The signal box lower left is Nine Mile Point No. 2; it had 36 levers.

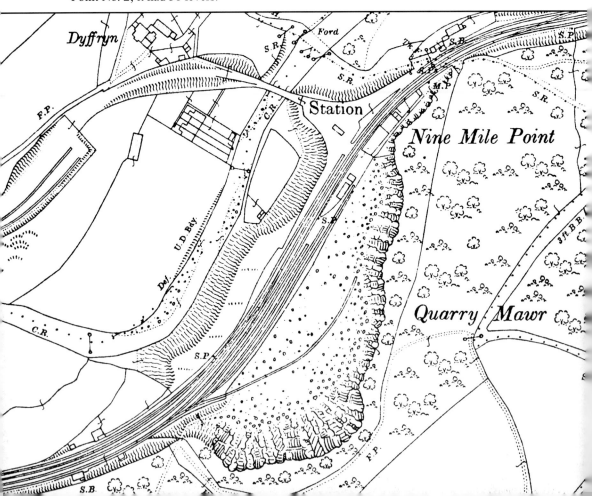

46.   This view is up the valley on 12th July 1958 and shows the natural charm of the locations between the industrialised regions. Goods and passenger services here were both withdrawn on 30th January 1959. The trackbed northwards from this area became part of the Sirhowy Valley Country Park. (H.C.Casserley)

PONT LAWRENCE HALT

47.   The station opened on 2nd October 1911 and it was termed a halt by the time it closed on 4th February 1957. Its location is shown on map XII. In the distance on this postcard is Nine Mile Point No. 1 box. (G.Davies coll.)

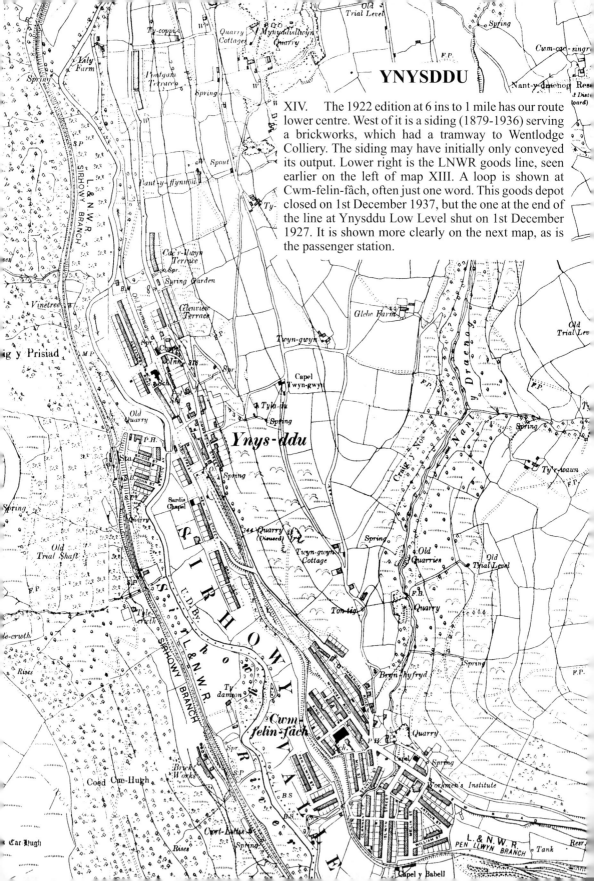

YNYSDDU

XIV.   The 1922 edition at 6 ins to 1 mile has our route lower centre. West of it is a siding (1879-1936) serving a brickworks, which had a tramway to Wentlodge Colliery. The siding may have initially only conveyed its output. Lower right is the LNWR goods line, seen earlier on the left of map XIII. A loop is shown at Cwm-felin-fâch, often just one word. This goods depot closed on 1st December 1937, but the one at the end of the line at Ynysddu Low Level shut on 1st December 1927. It is shown more clearly on the next map, as is the passenger station.

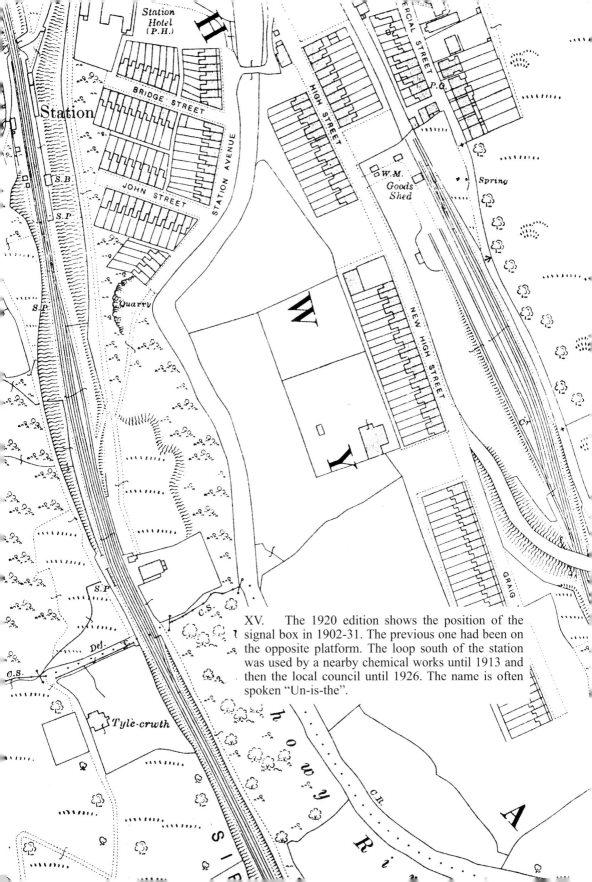

Station Hotel (P.H.)

Station

BRIDGE STREET

S.B.

JOHN STREET

S.P.

STATION AVENUE

S.P.

Quarry

S.P.

HIGH STREET

COMMERCIAL STREET

P.O.

W.M. Goods Shed

Spring

NEW HIGH STREET

Cr

GRAIG

S.P.

C.S.

Def.

O.S.

Tyle-crwth

XV.   The 1920 edition shows the position of the signal box in 1902-31. The previous one had been on the opposite platform. The loop south of the station was used by a nearby chemical works until 1913 and then the local council until 1926. The name is often spoken "Un-is-the".

48.   This indifferent northward view is from a tinted postcard and includes the signal box before the platforms were lengthened in front of it. (Lens of Sutton coll.)

49.   We look south on 12th July 1958 from above the road bridge. By that time, the facilities on the up platform totalled one lamp. (H.C.Casserley)

WYLLIE
HALT

50.   Seen   from
the down platform
on 12th July 1958
is Wyllie Colliery,
which   opened   in
1924. However, the
halt did not come
into use for the public
until 19th December
1932.
(R.M.Casserley)

51.   Recorded on
the same day was
0-6-0PT no. 3747
near No. 1 signal
box, which remained
in use until 20th
November 1967, as
did No. 2. This was
at the other end of the
complex of sidings,
which   functioned
until 9th September
1968. No. 1 had 18
levers and No. 2 had
20. (H.C.Casserley)

52.   The   cross-
over in the foreground
was retained until
June 1964. No. 9644
pauses on its way to
Risca on 7th May
1960, only weeks
before cessation of
passenger service.
(R.E.Toop)

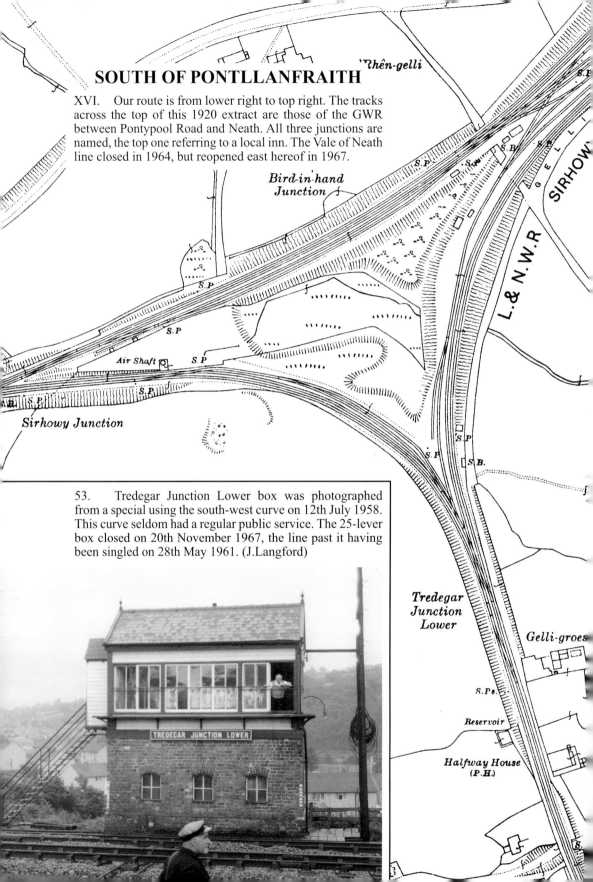

SOUTH OF PONTLLANFRAITH

'Rhên-gelli

XVI.   Our route is from lower right to top right. The tracks across the top of this 1920 extract are those of the GWR between Pontypool Road and Neath. All three junctions are named, the top one referring to a local inn. The Vale of Neath line closed in 1964, but reopened east hereof in 1967.

Bird-in-hand
Junction

S.B.

S.P.

S.P.

L. & N.W.R

SIRHOW

S.P

S.P

Air Shaft

S.P

Sirhowy Junction

S.P

S.B.

53.   Tredegar Junction Lower box was photographed from a special using the south-west curve on 12th July 1958. This curve seldom had a regular public service. The 25-lever box closed on 20th November 1967, the line past it having been singled on 28th May 1961. (J.Langford)

TREDECAR JUNCTION LOWER

Tredegar
Junction
Lower

Gelli-groes

S.Ps.

Reservoir

Halfway House
(P.H.)

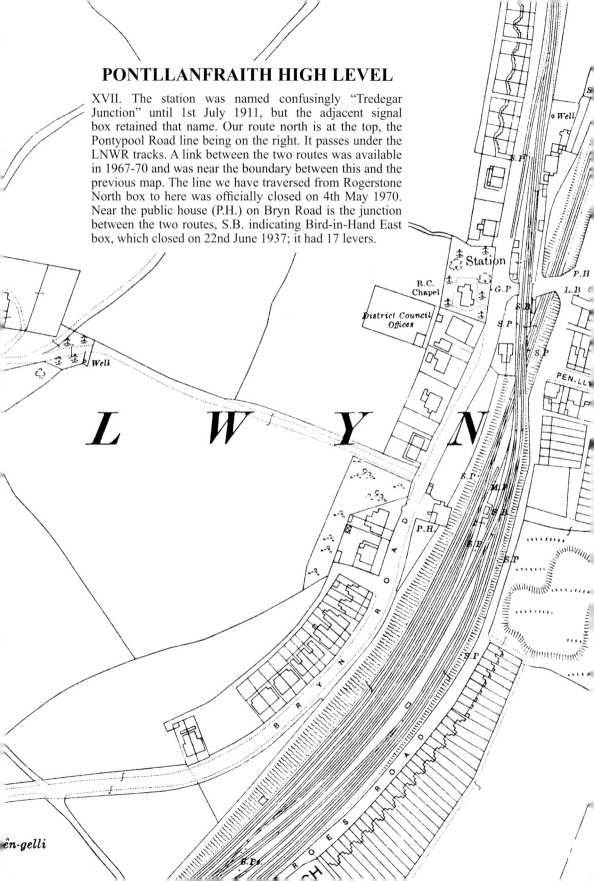

PONTLLANFRAITH HIGH LEVEL

XVII. The station was named confusingly "Tredegar Junction" until 1st July 1911, but the adjacent signal box retained that name. Our route north is at the top, the Pontypool Road line being on the right. It passes under the LNWR tracks. A link between the two routes was available in 1967-70 and was near the boundary between this and the previous map. The line we have traversed from Rogerstone North box to here was officially closed on 4th May 1970. Near the public house (P.H.) on Bryn Road is the junction between the two routes, S.B. indicating Bird-in-Hand East box, which closed on 22nd June 1937; it had 17 levers.

54.   This postcard was annotated *Tredegar Junction Station* and both platforms can be seen through the gates. The suffix HIGH LEVEL was used from 23rd May 1949.
(Lens of Sutton coll.)

Views of the junctions and Pontllanfraith Low Level station are to be found in pictures 48-55 in our *Pontypool to Mountain Ash* album.

---

55.   The obligatory fire buckets are hanging near the sign for GENTLEMEN, always a convenient source of fresh water. The look-out has his flag ready during repair work in about 1936. (Stations UK)

56.   The junction distant signals are in the background, as 0-8-0 no. 49316 trundles south with its tender cab keeping the flying coal dust and rain off the crew. The roof on the left had been damaged by a gas explosion in 1952. There had been a short siding in the road, near the bus, on the alignment of the Bryn Tramway. LMS freight trains began working as far south as Rogerstone Yard during World War II. (S.Rickard/J&J coll.)

57.   A southbound train departs and allows us sight of the footbridge which is not shown on the map. The bridge spans provided over the Neath lines are near the loco. The route had been doubled from Nine Mile Point in 1874. (H.C.Casserley)

58.   Bound for Ebbw Junction shed on 8th August 1959 are 0-8-0 no. 49064, with snowplough, and leading is no. 41204. Passing them is 0-6-2T no. 6641 with the 10.5am (Saturdays only) from Risca. It worked an excursion to Barry the next day. The signal box had a 38-lever frame. (S.Rickard/J&J coll.)

59.   The line was doubled northwards to Blackwood on 1st September 1891 and is seen on 7th May 1960 as 0-6-0PT no. 9644 waits with its short train, bound for Risca. Rochester pattern gas lights were in use to the end. (R.E.Toop)

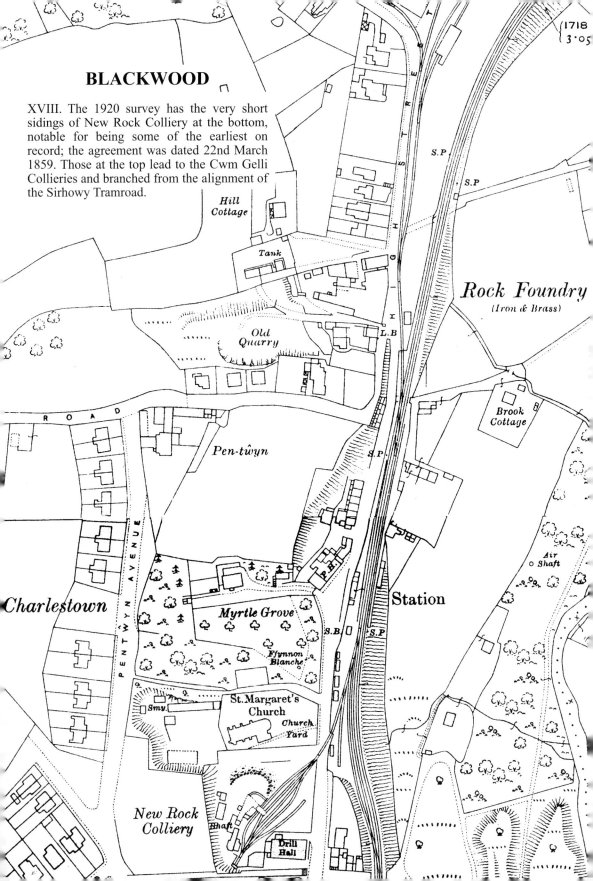

BLACKWOOD

XVIII. The 1920 survey has the very short sidings of New Rock Colliery at the bottom, notable for being some of the earliest on record; the agreement was dated 22nd March 1859. Those at the top lead to the Cwm Gelli Collieries and branched from the alignment of the Sirhowy Tramroad.

1718
3·05

Hill Cottage

Tank

S.P

S.P

Rock Foundry
(Iron & Brass)

Old Quarry

L.B

Brook Cottage

R O A D

Pen-tŵyn

S.P.

Air o Shaft

Charlestown

PENTWYN AVENUE

Myrtle Grove

Station

Ffynnon Blanche

S.B

S.P

Smy.

St. Margaret's Church

Church Yard

New Rock Colliery

Shaft

Drill Hall

60. An early southward view has the New Rock Colliery sidings packed with wagons. The sidings were in use for about 100 years. (Lens of Sutton coll.)

61. Again we look south, but from the down platform on 10th July 1958. Shown on the map, the dwelling on the left was just avoided by the surveyors. (H.C.Casserley)

62.　　No. 2 box (24 levers) was built in 1890 and was at the south end of the up platform; it was photographed in 1958. No. 1 (20 levers) was about ½ mile to the north and was open from 1914 until 1961. (H.C.Casserley)

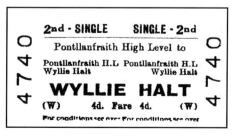

63.   The solid part of the platform is on the site of the original single short one and is seen in July 1959. The points to New Rock Colliery are unused. There is provision for gentlemen on both platforms. (H.C.Casserley)

64.   A straight length of track can be seen in the background as no. 9644 calls with a train for Risca on 7th May 1960. There was a siding for Primrose Colliery on the up side, about ¾ mile to the north, from 1890 to 1950. It was known as Rock Siding. (R.E.Toop)

NORTH OF BLACKWOOD

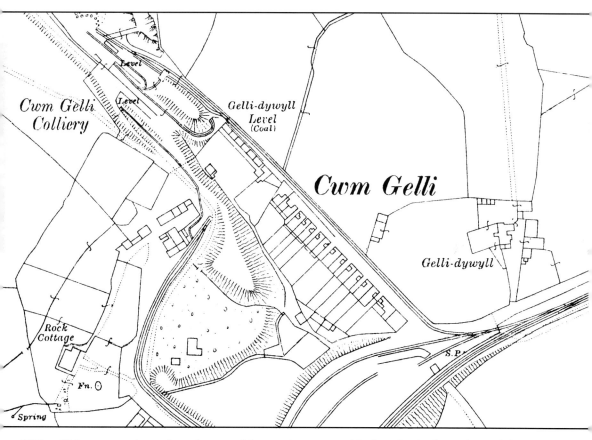

XIX.   This map continues from the top of the previous one and its location is shown lower left on the next one. The upper siding was in use from about 1912 to 1935.

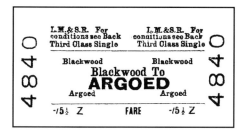

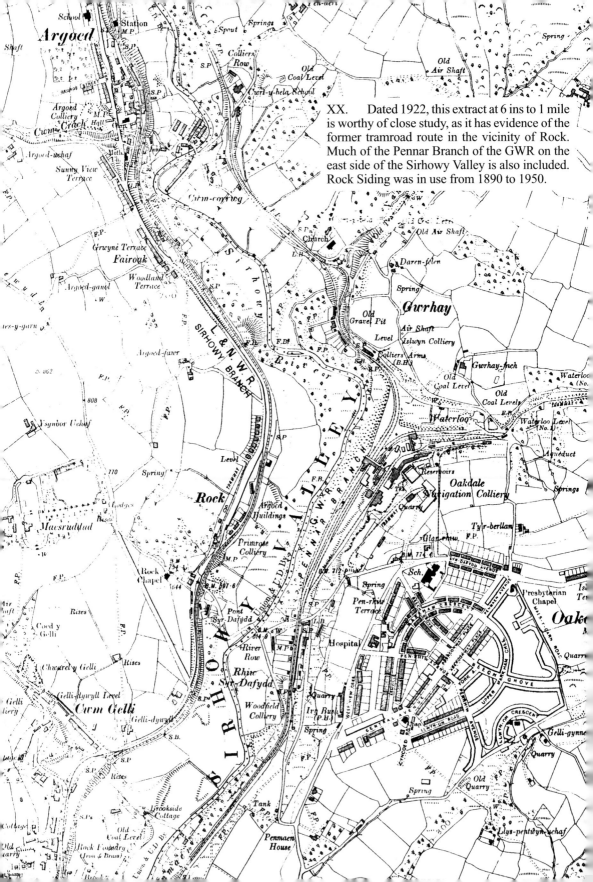

XX.   Dated 1922, this extract at 6 ins to 1 mile is worthy of close study, as it has evidence of the former tramroad route in the vicinity of Rock. Much of the Pennar Branch of the GWR on the east side of the Sirhowy Valley is also included. Rock Siding was in use from 1890 to 1950.

ARGOED HALT

XXI.   The High Street developed along the Sirhowy Tramroad, which was in or adjacent to the highway for much of its length. Railway conversion meant a new alignment east of the street, also a new straight road west of it and north of it, away from the new railway. As the new main road had to be higher on the valley side, there could not be a road link with the north end of the High Street, only a path. However, the output of Argoed Colliery (also known as Cwm Creeich Colliery) continued to be conveyed along the High Street until December 1916, when the straight connection (lower right) replaced the short curved siding for loading and new screens were built. The colliery closed in 1932 and it seems that the street tramway lasted until about that time. It would have been useful for local coal deliveries; it entered the goods yard at the top, through a gate.

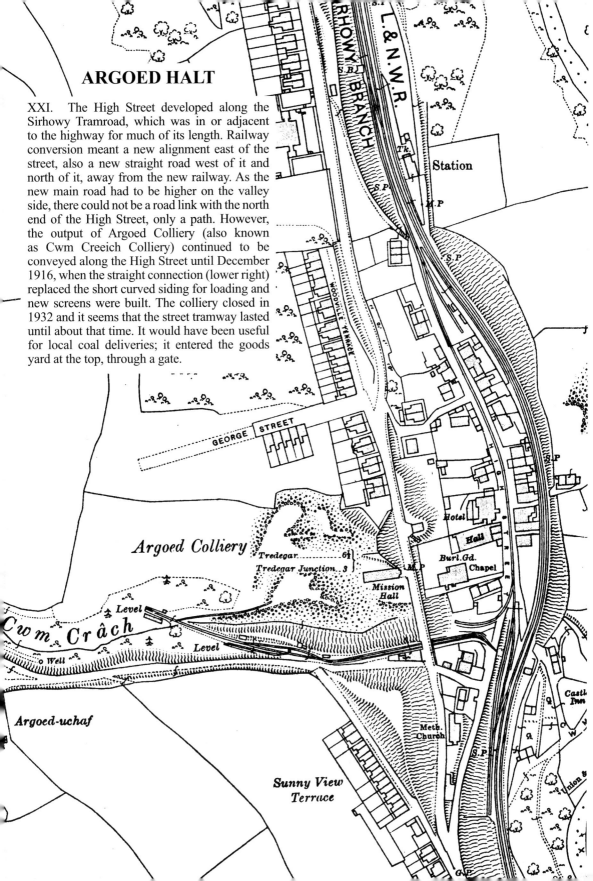

65.   Not many branches of Barclays Bank were situated on a historic mineral tramway and few will have seen it, other than locals, in this quiet street. (Postcard)

66.   A southward panorama includes the small goods yard and the High Street beyond it. The barrow crossing is between the two platforms. The building on the left dates from 1878 and is on the original platform. (Lens of Sutton coll.)

67.   No. 9644 waits with its single coach for Risca on 7th May 1960. The signal box (22 levers) had been built ready for the completion of double track, which came into use on 18th May 1890. (R.E.Toop)

68.   A 1961 landscape view shows that the High Street was eventually extended across the side of the goods yard, which closed with the passenger service in 1960. The station became a halt on 29th September 1941 and the down line was not used after 28th May 1961. (Stations UK)

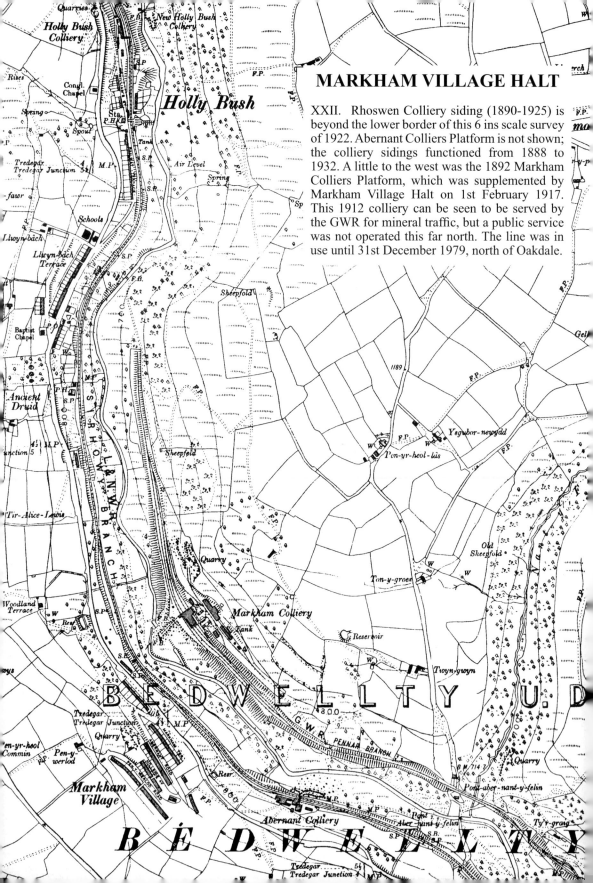

MARKHAM VILLAGE HALT

XXII. Rhoswen Colliery siding (1890-1925) is beyond the lower border of this 6 ins scale survey of 1922. Abernant Colliers Platform is not shown; the colliery sidings functioned from 1888 to 1932. A little to the west was the 1892 Markham Colliers Platform, which was supplemented by Markham Village Halt on 1st February 1917. This 1912 colliery can be seen to be served by the GWR for mineral traffic, but a public service was not operated this far north. The line was in use until 31st December 1979, north of Oakdale.

69.   A southward panorama in the vicinity of Abernant Colliery includes many of its owner's wagons, the identity of which was gradually lost during World War II due to the pooling arrangements. (Postcard)

70.   Class G2 0-8-0 no. 49409 is working an up workmens train on 27th April 1957 and is accelerating from the halt, which is in the background. It is climbing at 1 in 150.
(S.Rickard/P.Q.Treloar coll.)

71.   A close-up of the halt on 28th May 1960 reveals its simple construction and shows the footpath access on the up side. No. 6426 is hauling its usual single coach. (M.J.Stretton coll.)

72.   The remains of the halt are recorded in this 1961 northward view. The signal box was originally called Abernant No. 1 and had a 35-lever frame. It closed on 28th May 1961, when the route was singled. The sidings are round the curve and were in use between 1913 and 1961. On the left is Markham Colliery bath house. (Stations UK)

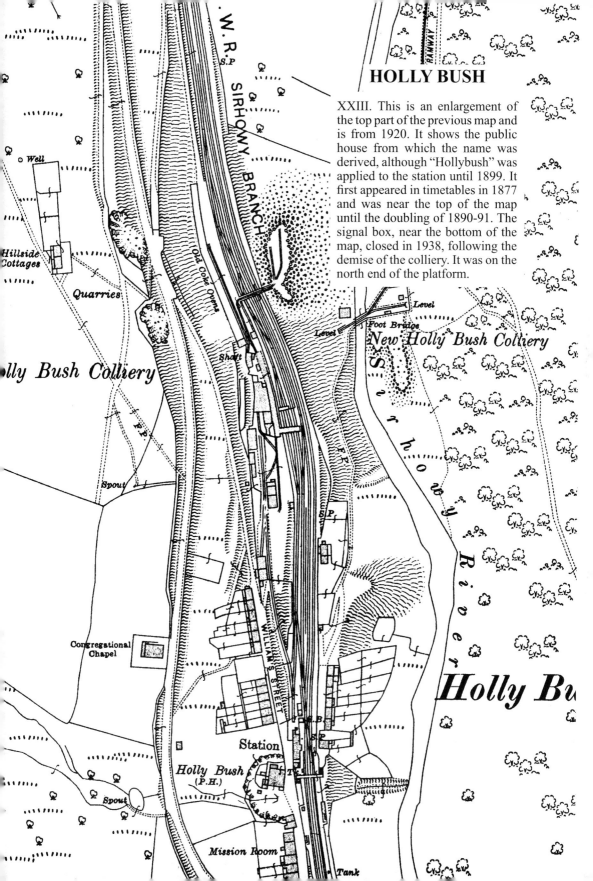

HOLLY BUSH

XXIII. This is an enlargement of the top part of the previous map and is from 1920. It shows the public house from which the name was derived, although "Hollybush" was applied to the station until 1899. It first appeared in timetables in 1877 and was near the top of the map until the doubling of 1890-91. The signal box, near the bottom of the map, closed in 1938, following the demise of the colliery. It was on the north end of the platform.

73.   The fire buckets are in the traditional location on the down platform, while a train stands at the up one in classic LNWR two-tone livery. (N.Seabourne coll.)

74.   Push-pull coach no. W246W is being propelled by a Pannier tank, sometime in the 1950s. Facilities for gentlemen have been removed, but the waiting shelter remains. (P.Q.Treloar coll.)

75.   Another Pannier tank is present as a more traditional ex-GWR autocoach waits at the
same platform. The waiting shelter carries the figures 1891. (Stations UK)

76.   Only days before closure to passengers, no. 3634 takes water near the barrow crossing.
The LMS hawks-eye nameboards remained at most stations in the valley. (E.Wilmshurst)

77.   The line had been doubled from Blackwood on 18th May 1890 and this was extended northward to Bedwellty Pits on 31st October 1891. The signal box had been on the right; the brick structure was probably its base. (Stations UK)

78.   "The Holly Bush" is seen with a seat outside in 1961 during the dismantling of the down platform. Only the up line was used after May of that year. (Stations UK)

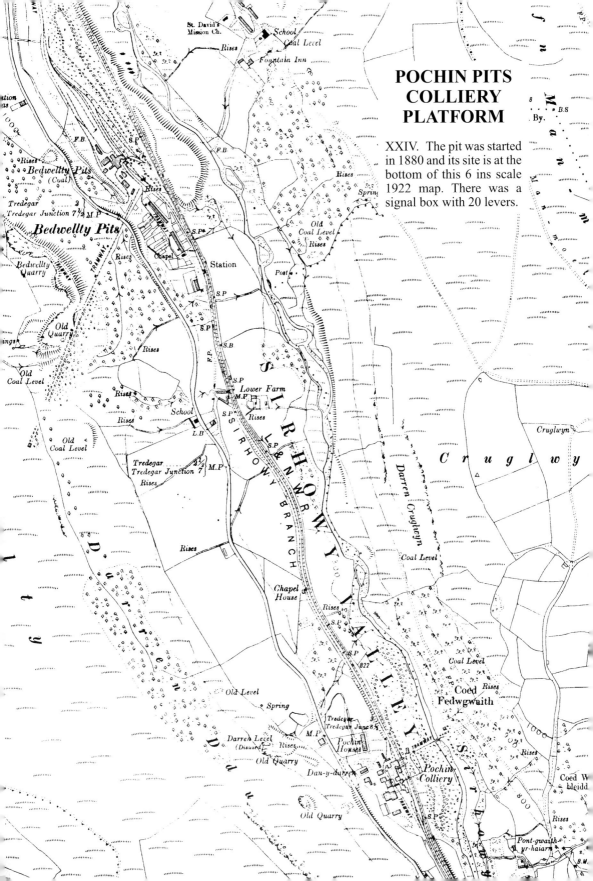

POCHIN PITS COLLIERY PLATFORM

XXIV. The pit was started in 1880 and its site is at the bottom of this 6 ins scale 1922 map. There was a signal box with 20 levers.

St. David's Mission Ch.
School
Coal Level
Rises
Fountain Inn

F.B.
Rises
Bedwellty Pits (Coal)
Rises
S.P.
Tredegar
Tredegar Junction 7½ M.P.
Bedwellty Pits
F.B.
Rises
Old Coal Level
Rises
Spring

Bedwellty Quarry
Rises
Chapel
S.P.
Station
Post
S.P.
Old Quarry
Rises
S.B.
Rises
Old Coal Level
Rises
S.P.
S.P.

Rises
S.P.
Lower Farm
M.P.
School
Rises
L.B.
S.P.
L.S. & N.W.
S.P.
Old Coal Level
Tredegar
Tredegar Junction 7½ M.P.
Rises
SIRHOWY VALLEY

Cruglwyn
Cruglwy

SIRHOWY BRANCH
Darren Cruglwyn
Coal Level

Rises
Chapel House
Rises
S.P.
Coal Level
822
S.P.
Coed Fedwgwaith
Rises

Old Level
Spring
M.P.
Darren Level (Disused)
Tredegar
Tredegar Junc 8¼
Old Quarry
Pochin Houses
Dan-y-darren
Pochin Colliery
Coed W bleidd
Rises

Old Quarry
S.P.
Pont-gwaith-yr-haiarn
B.M.

79. The up platform is evident in this undated view. The location appeared in public timetables from October 1893 until October 1922, but miners were accommodated until 1960. (Postcard)

80. The pit was owned by the Tredegar Iron & Coal Company until nationalisation and is seen on a card franked in 1963. Most of the landscape has now recovered from its industrial intrusion. (Postcard)

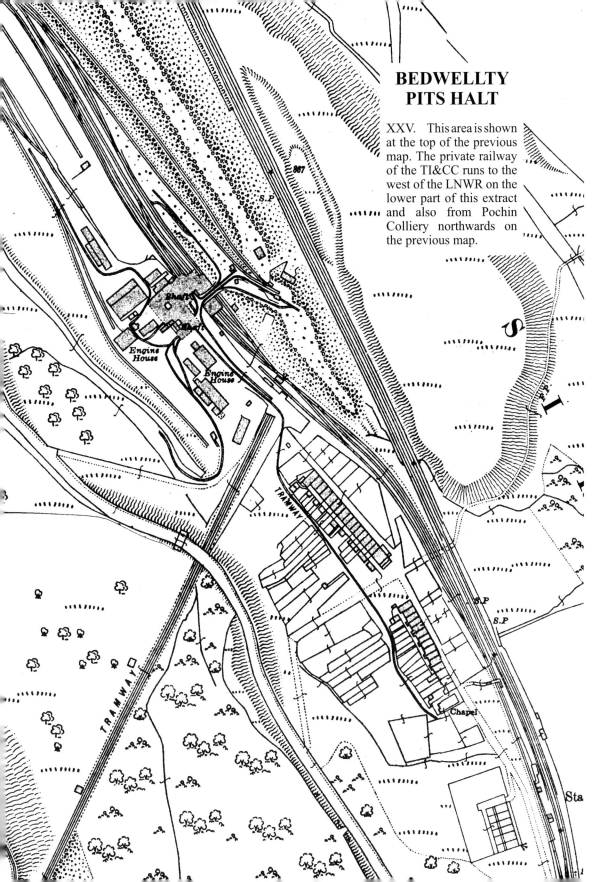

BEDWELLTY PITS HALT

XXV. This area is shown
at the top of the previous
map. The private railway
of the TI&CC runs to the
west of the LNWR on the
lower part of this extract
and also from Pochin
Colliery northwards on
the previous map.

81. The foot-bridge passed over the private line and can be seen on the map. We have two photographs of a "Coal Tank" 0-6-2T on 19th August 1950. (M.Whitehouse coll.)

82. This angle shows the unspoilt hillside in the background and the derelict trackbed of the former company lines in the foreground. There was a signal box nearby with 22 levers. (M.Whitehouse coll.)

83. The route from here to Tredegar was doubled in February 1875. The width of the valley is evident as no. 9644 calls on its way to Risca on 7th May 1960. On the right is Troedrhiwgair village. (R.E.Toop)

TREDEGAR

XXVI. The Tredegar Iron & Coal Company owned the lines on both sides of the LNWR in this region. It also controlled the pits, levels, drifts and industrial premises. Tredegar station is a little below centre on this 1922 extract, while Sirhowy station is near the top.

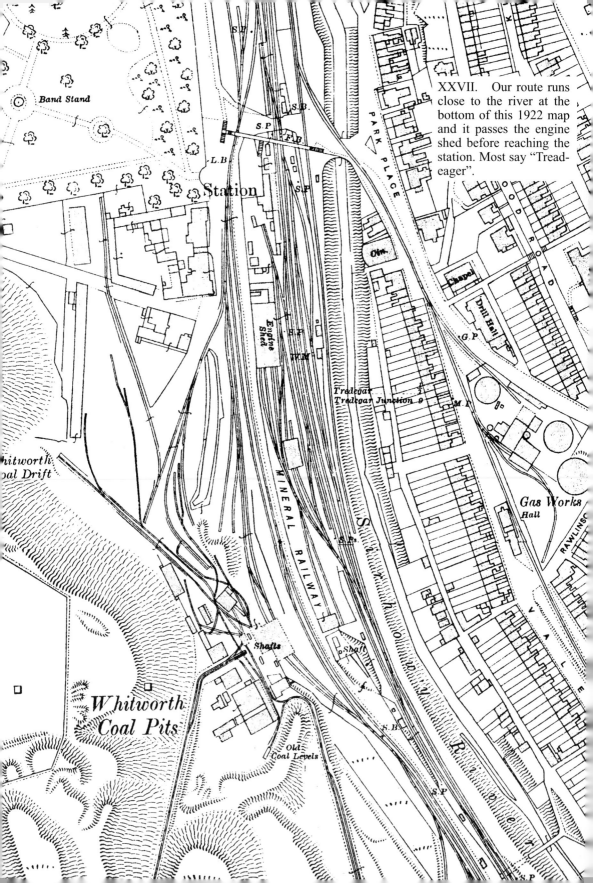

XXVII. Our route runs close to the river at the bottom of this 1922 map and it passes the engine shed before reaching the station. Most say "Tread-eager".

Band Stand

Station

PARK PLACE

Engine Shed

Tredegar
Tredegar Junction

Chapel

Drill Hall

G.P.

M.P.

Gas Works

Hall

Whitworth
Coal Drift

MINERAL RAILWAY

Shafts

Shaft

RAWLINSC

Whitworth
Coal Pits

Old
Coal Levels

S.B.

84.   An eastward view features the timber-clad station building before it was rebuilt in 1932. The posed group is standing on the tracks, which served the collieries to the south: Whitworth, Ty Trist and Bedwellty. (Postcard)

85.   This view south from the east end of the footbridge is before the 1922 rebuilding. Steam and smoke were everywhere in that period. Ty Trist coke ovens and colliery are in the background. (Lens of Sutton coll.)

86.   A northward panorama is from the vicinity of Whitworth Pits and features the engine shed (centre) and the water tank (lower right). The TI&CC tracks are in the foreground; its offices are on the left. (Lens of Sutton coll.)

87.   At almost 1000ft above sea level, rain frequently impaired photography. No. 6412 simmers on 7th August 1958, as an Austin A30 stands in the car park. Bedwellty Park offers a picturesque background. (G.Adams/M.J.Stretton coll.)

88.   Seen on the same day on the eastern siding is 0-8-0 no. 49421. On the right is the roof of the engine shed and in the distance is the South End colliers platform. (G.Adams/M.J.Stretton coll.)

89.   A rare view along the length of the single platform includes the low profile of a former Gwendraeth Valley Railway coach. Like other elderly vehicles, it was mainly for use by miners. The date is 16th July 1959. (H.C.Casserley)

90. Another 1959 photograph and this features coach cleaning, an inevitable problem with miners to convey. Unusual items of stock were often allocated here in semi-retirement. (S.Rickard/J&J coll.)

91. No. 9644 is about to depart for Risca on 7th May 1960. In the distance, the gradient rises at 1 in 54 for ½ mile towards Sirhowy. (R.E.Toop)

92.   Reference to the top of the last map will show that this footbridge passed over other railways on both sides of this one. No. 9644 is seen running round its coach after another trip on the same day. No. 1 Box (36 levers) closed on 28th May 1961. The goods yard (left) closed on 30th April 1969. (R.E.Toop)

93.   A view from the level crossing on 11th June 1960 has Middle Road to the left of the train and Goods Loop to the left of that. There was only single track to Sirhowy and that closed on 4th November 1963. No. 3634 is working the 3.37 from Risca to Nantybwch. (E.Wilmshurst)

Tredegar Engine Shed

94. The allocation at the end of 1947 was one Ivatt LMS 2-6-2T and ex-LNWR locos thus: seven 0-6-2Ts, two 0-8-4Ts and six 0-8-0s. All were removed at the end of February 1950, but in November 1954, 21 engines arrived, mainly of the types mentioned. This is the scene soon after. (R.M.Casserley)

95. Ex-GWR engines began to appear during 1958, such as 0-6-0PT no. 5737, seen on 16th July. Also visible is No. 2 Box (30 levers), which closed the same day as No. 1. The colliers platform is seen in full. (H.C.Casserley)

96. Ex-LMS 2-6-2T no. 41204 was recorded on the same day. The shed had lost three sections of its roof in a fire on 20th March 1910 and the damaged parts were partially removed. The coal stage is in the background. (H.C.Casserley)

97.   The same loco was photographed at the coal stage on 8th August of the same year. The LMS code of 4E was retained until 1950 and 86K was used from 1954. (S.Rickard/J&J coll.)

98.   On shed on the same day was 0-6-0PT no. 6412 and 2-6-2T no. 41201. The shed roof was never repaired and all locos were removed when passenger services ceased. (S.Rickard/J&J coll.)

NORTH OF TREDEGAR

99. The station is in the distance in this southward view of the National Coal Board's yard on 2nd September 1957. Featured is 0-4-0ST no. 5, which was built by Hawthorn Leslie in 1900. A special train is standing on the main line.
(M.Dart coll.)

100. Another view towards the station and this includes the well groomed BR siding, plus overgrown NCB lines. The new building near the van was erected on the site of the cattle pens.
(D.K.Jones coll.)

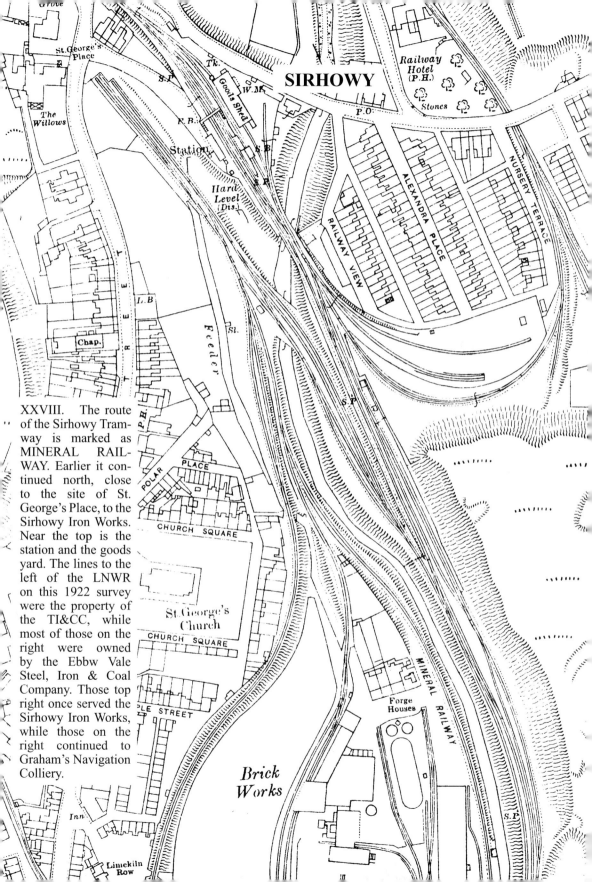

SIRHOWY

Grove

St. George's Place

The Willows

Railway Hotel (P.H.)

Stones

P.O.

Tk.

S.I.

Goods Shed

W.M.

F.B.

S.B.

Station

S.B.

ALEXANDRA PLACE

NURSERY TERRACE

Hard Level (Dis.)

RAILWAY VIEW

L.B

Chap.

Feeder

Sl.

S.P.

P.H.

POLAR PLACE

CHURCH SQUARE

St. George's Church

CHURCH SQUARE

MINERAL RAILWAY

PLE STREET

Forge Houses

Brick Works

Inn

Limekiln Row

S.P.

XXVIII. The route of the Sirhowy Tramway is marked as MINERAL RAILWAY. Earlier it continued north, close to the site of St. George's Place, to the Sirhowy Iron Works. Near the top is the station and the goods yard. The lines to the left of the LNWR on this 1922 survey were the property of the TI&CC, while most of those on the right were owned by the Ebbw Vale Steel, Iron & Coal Company. Those top right once served the Sirhowy Iron Works, while those on the right continued to Graham's Navigation Colliery.

101.   Graham Brothers Ltd later owned the colliery and its navigation coal was ideal for ships. It closed in 1926 and its location is marked just above the centre of map no. XXVI. (Postcard)

102.   The main building was on the up side and was timber framed throughout the life of the line. However, the height of the platform was increased in later years. The name is usually spoken "Sear-how-ee". On the left is the LNWR signal box. (Lens of Sutton coll.)

103.   A southward view includes both the goods shed and the signal box, which had been moved in 1927. The gradient post indicates an increase from 1 in 52 to 1 in 37. Most of the remainder of the journey was up at 1 in 42. (Lens of Sutton coll.)

104.   Moving back a few yards and on a few years, we see the LMS sign still in place in 1958, ten years after the company had ceased to exist. Note the unusual lamp, centre. The bidirectional goods loop runs between the goods shed and the platform. (R.M.Casserley)

105.   Moving to the south end of the platform, still in 1958, we glimpse the gate on the trackbed of the private line that once ran east. It carried the Ebbw Vale Company's siding and was later leased to Graham Brothers. The line that ran between the back of the down platform and the goods shed provided a bi-directional goods loop. It was used for coal from Rickard's Level, which was on the site of the Sirhowy Ironworks. The line north to Nantybwch closed completely on 13th June 1960. (R.M.Casserley)

106.   The final shot was taken not long before closure to passengers. Goods traffic continued until 4th November 1963, when the line from Tredegar closed completely. The signal box closed on 28th May 1961, its frame having 50 levers. Note that the goods shed had been extended. (M.J.Stretton coll.)

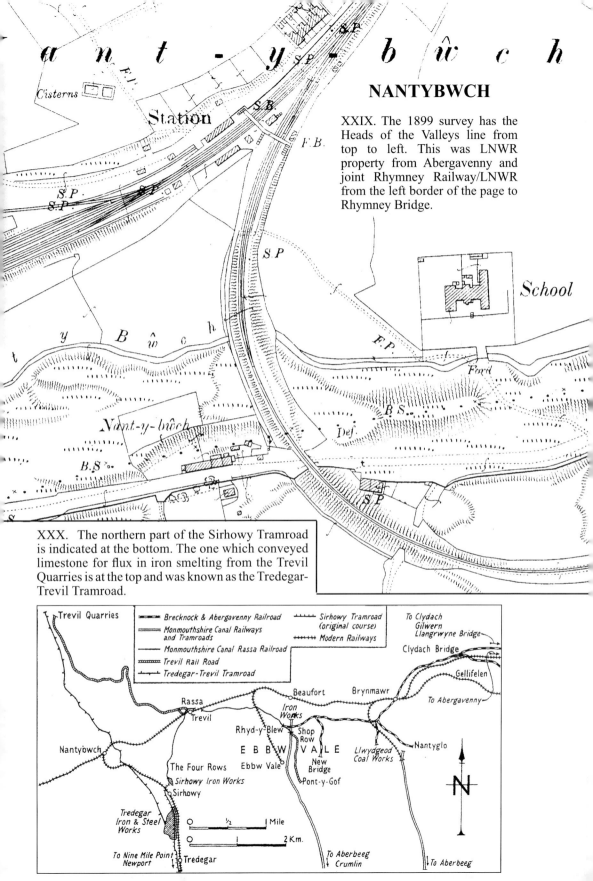

NANTYBWCH

XXIX. The 1899 survey has the Heads of the Valleys line from top to left. This was LNWR property from Abergavenny and joint Rhymney Railway/LNWR from the left border of the page to Rhymney Bridge.

XXX. The northern part of the Sirhowy Tramroad is indicated at the bottom. The one which conveyed limestone for flux in iron smelting from the Trevil Quarries is at the top and was known as the Tredegar-Trevil Tramroad.

107.   Nos 7710 and 27654 are seen with the 9.05am from Newport on 26th April 1948. The leading engine was on its way to another duty and coupled to a scheduled train to reduce single line occupancy. (W.A.Camwell)

108.   Another of the 0-6-2T "Coal Tanks" was recorded on 19th August 1950, waiting to return to Newport. The need for coal rails is evident. (M.Whitehouse coll.)

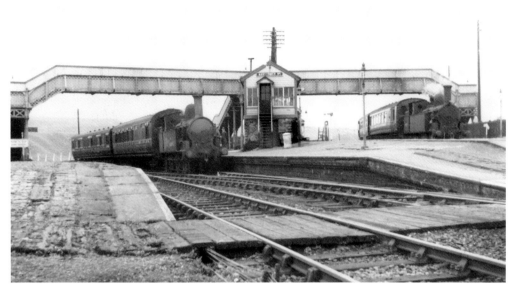

109.   Recorded on the same day was 0-6-2T no. 7752 (left) with a train from Newport and sister engine no. 58933 with one from Merthyr, but no passengers are evident. Nantybwch No. 1 signal box is prominent between the two trains. (M.Whitehouse coll.)

110.   The "Coal Tanks" were predominant on the former LMS routes in Monmouthshire. No. 58925 was photographed after having run round its train on the same day. (M.Whitehouse coll.)

111.   The influence of BR was slow coming to this remote part of the network. However, ex-LMS no. 40097 had been relettered before the lion and monocycle became common. The footbridge was still boarded on 13th May 1954. (T.J.Edgington)

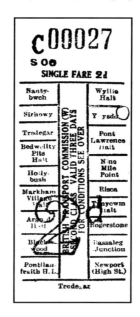

112.   A miners train nears the top of the incline on 14th August 1957, headed by 0-6-0PT no. 4643 and banked by 2-6-2T no. 40171. The train has climbed to an altitude of 1165ft above sea level. (S.Rickard/J&J coll.)

113.   The No. 1 Box was completed in 1891 and was in use until 1959, when the route eastward closed. The Heads of the Valleys passenger service ceased on 6th January 1958. (S.Rickard/J&J coll.)

114.   Rounding the final curve is a miners train from the Sirhowy Valley on 14th August 1957; no. 41204 is in charge. The contorted landscape is evidence of prolonged industrial activity in the area. The platform on the left was only used by an occasional excursion train. (S.Rickard/J&J coll.)

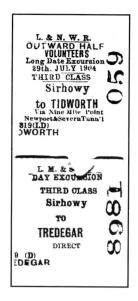

115.   Seen on the same day is 0-6-0PT no. 6423 with an Abergavenny to Merthyr service in poor light. Thick cloud was often a problem here, but at least the tree-less rolling hills can be enjoyed. (S.Rickard/J&J coll.)

116.   The platform for trains from Merthyr is featured, along with part of the dock, on the left. There was vehicular access to the north side of the building, albeit by an unsurfaced single track lane. The structure included the ticket office and porters room. (D.Edge coll.)

117.   We move on to 26th October 1957 and can enjoy the sight of 0-8-0 no. 49409 waiting with a miners train in the goods sidings adjacent to the double track. The short headshunt on the right led to the little-used local goods siding. On the left is No. 2 Box, which is thought to be of Rhymney Railway origin, as it was stone built. The sidings continued to be used for stabling and running round stock after the closure of the line westwards. (G.Adams/M.J.Stretton coll.)

118.   The end is nigh on 5th January 1958 as one man and his dog ponder the merits of a photograph of empty platforms. It enables us to savour the atmosphere of this desolate location, where even the protective boards on the footbridge had gone. The low cloud is formed by the exhaust of the last train to Merthyr. (H.C.Casserley)

119.   This is the final day of operation, 11th June 1960. The northern platforms had been out of use for 2½ years and the one on the left had seldom been used. There had been a rare Saturday excursion from Brynmawr to Barry Island which stopped at it. No. 3634 has just arrived with the 4.32pm from Tredegar; the last up train. (E.Wilmshurst)

120.   On the other end of the final train was no. 8711. The last departure from this junction, much loved by rural railway admirers, was at 4.50pm. (D.K.Jones coll.)

Other views of this station can be seen in illustrations 85 to 93 in *Abergavenny to Merthyr.*

MP Middleton Press

EVOLVING THE ULTIMATE RAIL ENCYCLOPEDIA

Easebourne Lane, Midhurst, West Sussex.
GU29 9AZ   Tel:01730 813169

www.middletonpress.co.uk   email:info@middletonpress.co.uk

A-0 906520   B-1 873793   C-1 901706   D-1 904474

OOP Out of print at time of printing - Please check availability   BROCHURE AVAILABLE SHOWING NEW TITLES